For
My   Parents
and
Alan   and   Alexander

Fairness in Personnel Selection

An organizational justice perspective

M. SINGER
University of Canterbury, New Zealand

Avebury

Aldershot · Brookfield USA · Hong Kong · Singapore · Sydney

Published by
Avebury
Ashgate Publishing Limited
Gower House
Croft Road
Aldershot
Hants GU11 3HR
England

Ashgate Publishing Company
Old Post Road
Brookfield
Vermont 05036
USA

A CIP catalogue record for this book is available from the British Library.

ISBN 1 85628 475 1

Printed and Bound in Great Britain by
Athenaeum Press Ltd, Newcastle upon Tyne.

Contents

1 Introduction

The core subject matter of personnel selection research consists of job analysis, criterion and predictor measurement, as well as validity and utility issues. Research on each of these topics has focused primarily on the improvement of accuracy in predicting job performance and thereby increasing the rate of valid selections.

Valid selections involve the use of job-relevant qualifications and hence are merit-based. Utility analyses have consistently shown that such merit-based selection procedures can significantly increase organizational productivity (e.g., Cascio, 1982, 1991; Schmidt et. al., 1979; Schmidt et al., 1992; Schmitt & Noe, 1986). Research into the development of valid selection procedures is therefore aiming at optimising human resources utilisation with the ultimate goal of maximising organizational productivity and effectiveness.

From this point of view, valid selections would serve the organization well. However, from the applicants' perspective, some rather different issues come to the fore. The most important one concerns the fairness of the selection. Social psychological research has shown that justice is the central concern of human beings (e.g., Lerner, 1982) and that in situations involving the allocation of resources, individuals' attention is drawn primarily to the question of equity (e.g., Lind & Tyler, 1988). In a selection context whereby employment opportunities are allocated, job candidates are likely to seek answers to questions such as "How was the decision made?" or "Did the best qualified person get the job?" Both questions concern fairness: The former addresses the fairness of the selection procedures and the latter, the fairness of the

1

selection outcome.

But why do candidates attach such importance to the fairness of selection? One obvious reason is that candidates have vested interest in the selection outcomes in terms of their own career prospects. At the present time of diminishing economic resources and shrinking employment opportunities, selection outcomes may have even greater significant and far-reaching consequences for the candidates. Here concern for selection fairness thus stems from one's self-interest. This self-interest notion is implicit in existing justice theories (i.e., Thibaut & Walker, 1975; Leventhal, 1980; Lind & Tyler, 1988).

A second reason takes a group perspective. It has been argued that "procedures" adopted by a group (or organization) represent norms of the group's structures and processes and hence are the manifestations of the values of the group (Lind & Tyler, 1988). In the selection context, selection procedures adopted by the recruiting organization would be seen by candidates as being indicative of the general values and norms of the organization. Because information about organizational values is crucial in their evaluation of the organisation as a prospective employer, job candidates are therefore concerned with the justice of the organization's selection practices.

From the perspective of the recruiting organization, although it is the validity of the selection *per se* that directly impacts on its productivity and effectiveness, there are good reasons for the organization to place high, if not equal, importance on the fairness of its selection practice. First, psychometric evidence based on utility analyses has shown that the selection procedures accepted as "the most fair" (i.e., Cleary's regression model), are also the ones that yield the highest utility value in the dollar estimation of organizational productivity (e.g., Hartigan & Wigdor, 1989; Hunter et al., 1977; Schmidt et al., 1984; Schmitt, 1989). In other words, the most fair method of selection also appears to be the most valid in terms of organizational productivity and effectiveness.

The second reason for an organization to give high priority to the fairness of its selection practice concerns its role in society. As organizations are part of the social community, they have moral obligations and responsibilities for the society as a whole. If the main goal of the society is to achieve equal opportunity for just and fair competitions among individuals, organisations are then morally bound in helping fostering such a goal by ensuring the use of fair criteria in their selection practices.

Another reason concerns the organization's overall image to

2

the public. In the context of the group value argument mentioned earlier (Lind & Tyler, 1988), as selection prodecures are seen as reflecting the overriding values and norms of the organization, they are therefore an indirect means of projecting a (favorable) public image.

Having established the importance of the fairness in personnel selection, two questions follow logically:"What are the determinants of a fair selection practice?" and "What are the consequences of a fair (or unfair) selection practice?". The rest of the book presents empirical data from relevant studies designed to address specific issues pertaining to these two general questions. The conceptual basis for these studies stems from current organizational justice theories.

Since the mid-1980s, rapid advancement in organizational justice theories has been made with reference to distributive justice (Deutsch, 1985; Lansberg, 1989), procedural justice (Lind & Tyler, 1988) and related notions of justice including interactional justice (Bies, 1987b; Tyler & Bies, 1990) and scope of justice (e.g., Tyler & Lind, 1990). The theoretical advancement has stimulated ample research into a variety of justice issues in organizational settings. Examples of such issues include conflict resolution (e.g., Karambayya & Brett, 1989), grievance management (e.g., Klaas. 1989), pay equity (e.g., Jackson, 1989), promotion practices (e.g., McEuruc, 1989) and employee layoffs (e.g., Brockner, 1990). These studies have proved that current organizational justice theories can provide a comprehensive and integrative conceptual framework in the examination of justice or fairness issues in organizations. However, in the context of selection practices, selection fairness research has so far been examined from a psychometric and utility perspective, little effort has been made in systematically applying the justice theoretical framework to selection research.

This book intends to advocate such an application to selection fairness research. This approach would serve two unique purposes: The first is to enhance understanding of issues of selection fairness from the perspective of current organizational justice theories. In particular, fairness associated with both selection outcomes and selection procedures. Selection fairness research taking this perspective would have its focus on ethical and social justice concerns, readily distinguishable from its traditional psychometric and utility emphasis. The second purpose is to allow a systematic examination of possible behavioural consequences of a fair or unfair selection practice within the theoretical contexts of relevant justice theories, since most outcome and procedural justice theories

3

postulate on behavioural consequences of injustice.

To this end, the book will first present a review of current organizational justice theories and a review of selection fairness research. It will then identify areas in selection research to which the conceptual framework of justice theories could fruitfully be applied. In doing so, the limited available research that has taken such an approach will be reported.

✳ Chapter two presents a review of organizational justice theories and research. The review covers recent literature on distributive (or outcome) justice, procedural justice, interactional justice, and other developments in justice notions including the provision of justifications, fabrications of justice, the scope of justice and the psychology of improving justice.

✳ Chapter three reviews the selection fairness literature to date and covers fairness issues associated with the use of both tests and interviews as predictors of selection. With reference to test use, the review includes psychometric issues of test validation, the development of test fairness models, test utility and issues of subgroup ability differences. With reference to selection interviews, research findings of various sources of bias in interview decision making are reviewed.

Chapter four deals with the application of the procedural justice framework to selection research. It is argued that procedural justice notions could be applied to the identification of fairness determinants of selection procedures, as well as to the examination of possible consequences of candidates' fairness perceptions about selection procedures. Relevant research findings are reported. First, determinants of fair selection procedures for both entry-level and managerial selection are identified. These determinants are reviewed with reference to Leventhal, Karuza and Fry's (1980) theory of allocation preference. Second, the chapter examines evidence on the effects of successful candidates' fairness perceptions about selection procedures on their later job behaviour and attitudes.

Chapter five focuses on the application of distributive justice framework to selection research. Because the distributive justice notion is most relevant to preferential selection (or quota hiring), this chapter then concentrates on the outcome justice of preferential selection. The chapter first reports recent studies on outcome justice perceptions about gender-based and ethnicity-based preferential selection. Because these findings are convergent in showing that outcomes of preferential selection are perceived as unfair, it is proposed that these findings can best be interpreted

4

within the conceptual framework of the theory of relative deprivation. The chapter then examines the application of relative deprivation theory to outcome justice in preferential selection. Within this framework, the chapter finally discusses possible behavioural consequences of preferential selection.

Chapter six examines the effect of the provision of justifications to fairness judgements of preferential selection. Three studies designed to test the effect are reported. Contrary to existing literature on the fairness-enhancing effect of justification, it has been found that the provision of justification for preferential selection decisions further exacerbated perceptions of injustice. Several likely reasons for the inconsistency in the justification effect are then discussed.

In conclusion, chapter seven summaries existing literature on the application of organizational justice framework to selection fairness research. The chapter further identifies areas in selection research whereby such an application would be useful. These include the application of interactional justice notion to fairness issues in selection interviews, the examination of the justification effect and the scope of justice effect in outcome fairness perceptions of preferential selection, and finally, the application of Cook's (1990) concept of the psychology of improving justice to selection fairness research.

2 Theories of organizational justice

For decades, organizational researchers have been concerned with issues of fairness and justice. Prior to the 1980s, the most dominant conceptual framework for organizational justice research was that based on equity theories (Adams, 1965; Walster, Berscheid & Walster, 1973). Empirical research then focused primarily on the fairness of monetary and non-monetary rewards (e.g., Campbell & Pritchard, 1976; Goodman & Friedman, 1971; Weick, 1966). The 1980s saw an expansion of organizational justice research, both in theory development and empirical investigations.

In a comprehensive review, Greenberg (1987a) categorised organizational justice theories according to two dimensions: a reactive-proactive dimension and a process-content dimension. The former dimension distinguishes reactive justice theories, dealing with individuals' reactions to injustice, from those proactive theories attempting to prescribe means to attain justice.

Examples of Reactive and Proactive Justice Theories

Equity theory is a good example of a reactive theory as it has postulated various actions an individual might take when faced with inequity. According to Adams (1965), equity perception involves a comparison between one's own "reward/effort" (outcome/input) ratio to that of a referent person. When an individual perceives that he/she is underrewarded, the person may react by lowering his/her effort, or seeking to increase the reward, or cognitively distorting the input/output ratio, or substituting the referent person for comparison, or simply quitting the field. Reactive justice theories thus examine people's reactions in an

6

attempt to reddress justice.

Another example of a reactive theory is the theory of relative deprivation (Davies, 1959; Pettigrew, 1978; Runciman, 1966). The theory contends that unfavourable outcomes of social comparisons may produce feelings of deprivation and discontent which in turn may give rise to behavioural consequences that are either individual-oriented (e.g., lowered self-esteem or other symptoms of helplessness) or system-oriented (e.g., social unrest or riots) (Crosby, 1982, 1984; Martin, 1981).

While reactive theories focus on reactions to injustice, proactive theories set out to promote justice by examining and designing means to achieve justice. For instance, justice is conceptualised as a basic human motive by Lerner (1982). In his justice motive theory, Lerner (1982) has further postulated four general rules for fair resources allocations: allocations based on the parity principle, on relative contributions, on performance outcome or on relative needs. Several other proactive theories also attempt to specify the criteria of either fair allocations (e.g., Deutsch, 1985; Leventhal, 1976; 1980), or fair allocation procedures (e.g., Leventhal, Karuza & Fry, 1980). The second dimension used by Greenberg (1987a) in categorising justice theories concerned the process-content dichotomy. Here, Greenberg made the distinction between process and content theories of justice. Process theories concern procedural justice or the fairness of the processes used to determine the final outcome of an allocation. Content theories, on the other hand, focus on distributive justice or the fairness of the final outcome of an allocation.

In a more recent review, Greenberg (1990a) presented a historical overview of the field of organizational justice and made the plea for the improvement of research methodology as well as the integration of disparate but similar concepts in the field. Since Greenberg's two reviews (1987a, 1990a), rapid advancement has been made in theory and empirical research with reference to both outcome and procedural justice, as well as in other concepts of justice including interactional justice, the provision of justifications, fabrications of injustice, scope of justice and the psychology of improving justice. The rest of the chapter presents a review of these recent developments.

Outcome Justice: Theories and Empirical Findings

Earlier organizational research on distributive or outcome justice has been dominated by propositions derived from equity theory (for

7

a review, see Mowday, 1987). Although the conceptual basis for several recent studies examining issues of organizational justice still stemms from equity theory (e.g., Dornstein, 1989; Greenberg, 1989, 1990b; Griffeth, Vecchio & Logan, 1989), the theory has become less popular since the mid-1980s (Furby, 1986; Reis, 1986).

The inadequacies of equity theories as a conceptual framework for organizational justice research have been noted by several researchers (e.g., Folger, 1986a; Locke & Henne, 1986; Miles, Hatfield & Huseman, 1989). These inadequacies include first, the definition of inequity solely as a social comparison in terms of the outcome/input ratio, second, the neglect of procedural justice notion, and third, the lack of specificity in the prediction of individuals' reactions to perceived injustice. In addressing these inadequacies, Folger (1986a, 1986b) has proposed a referent cognitions theory (RCT). Within the RCT framework, injustice is conceptualised as a result of a hypothetical comparison process rather than a social comparison between two persons. The hypothetical comparison involves a comparison between a state of reality and a state of imaginable referent (i.e., a referent cognition or what might have been instead). The RCT framework also made provisions for the procedural justice notion by way of the assumption that outcomes are evaluated against all "possible circumstances that are instrumental in producing the outcomes" (i.e., the "instrumentalities"). Empirical research generated from the referent cognitions theory of justice are in general supportive of the theory (e.g., Ambrose et al., 1991; Cropanzano & Folger, 1989; Folger & Konovsky, 1989).

The theory of relative deprivation mentioned earlier in the context of reactive justice theories, is another outcome justice theory that has recently received considerable attention in organizational justice research. The theory was originally advanced for social political and economical problems (Davies, 1959; Gurr, 1970; Pettigrew, 1967). Relative deprivation theory is concerned with first, an individual's (or individuals') feelings of deprivation resulting from comparing his or her (or their) rewards with those of a comparative referent person (or group); and second, the behavioral effects of such feelings of deprivation. The theory makes the distinction between egoistic deprivation and fraternal or group deprivation (Rhodebeck, 1981; Runciman, 1966; Crosby, 1984). Egoistic deprivation occurs as a result of a comparison between two individuals (Crosby, 1976). Fraternal deprivation refers to the discontent stemming from the status of the entire group to which

8

an individual belongs as compared to a referent group.

Several advances of the relative deprivation concept have been made. Crosby (1984) has proposed that the notions of "wanting" and "deserving" be incorporated into the definition of the relative deprivation construct. Applying the referent cognitions concept, Folger (1986b) argued that feelings of relative deprivation could also be a result of an individual's referent cognitions in terms of "what would/should have been". In the context of a social categorisation theory of entitlement, Lansberg (1989) conceptualises fraternal deprivation as a result of applying illegitimate criteria in deriving differential group entitlements. With reference to the application of relative deprivation theory to pay inequity research, Wegener (1990) found that people's perceptions about social economical distributions were distorted as a result of the levelling vs. sharpening processes in social hierachy perceptions. Wegener argued that the observed misperceptions about social distributions create illusory justice evaluations and hence relative deprivation research would have to take account of this general perceptual phenomenon.

In terms of empirical research, early relative deprivation studies reported evidence of deprivation based on racial (e.g., Sears & McConahay, 1970; Vanneman & Pettigrew, 1972) and gender inequities (e.g., Crosby, 1982, 1984; Martin, 1981). The concept of relative deprivation has recently been applied to organizational issues including pay satisfaction (deCarufel, 1986; Sweeney, McFarlin & Inderrieden, 1990), sex-based pay inequities (Dornstein, 1989; Jackson, 1989) as well as deprivation concerning employment and career opportunities (Tougas & Veilleux, 1988, 1989; Veilleux & Tougas, 1989).

Several other outcome justice theories focus primarily on the key determinants of a fair outcome of a distribution or allocation. Lerner's (1977, 1982) justice motive theory mentioned previously as an example of a proactive theory, identifies four criteria for a fair resources allocation (i.e., criteria based on performance, equality, contributions and needs). The application of these criteria are, however, situation-specific. Leventhal's (1976, 1980) justice judgement theory also identifies different rules of fair allocations for different social situations. The norms for distributive justice in these theories therefore vary according to the characteristics of the situation, particularly social relations among recipients of the allocation.

A similar emphasis on social relations can be found in

9

Deutsch's (1985) conception of distributive justice. Based on his own work on distributive justice over the last 40 years, Deutsch (1985) concluded that in social situations emphasising corporation rather than competition, just allocations typically are based on the parity principle (i.e., equal allocations regardless of contribution, performance or needs). This rule of allocation also has more favorable effects on recipient wellbeing, social relations as well as group productivity. More recently, Meindl (1989) identifies the social conditions under which leaders are likely to adopt either a parity or an equity rule in making a fair resources allocation.

In the context of outcome justice, Lansberg (1989) examined the cognitive underpinnings of individuals' justice perceptions of the entitlements they receive in exchange for their group membership and contributions to an organization. Lansberg's three-step justice model contends that justice perceptions of an individual's entitlement depend on the outcomes of a group categorization process in establishing his/her group membership status, a social comparison process involving similar referents, and a social contrast process involving dissimilar referents.

Procedural Justice: Theories and Empirical Findings

Traditional approach to justice issues in organizations concentrate primarily on distributive or outcome justice. However, stimulated by Thibaut and Walker's (1975, 1978) original work on the justice of legal procedures, organizational researchers have since taken an increasing interest in issues of procedural justice. In the context of the processes of legal dispute resolution, Thibaut and Walker identified "process control" and "decision control" as the key determinants of procedural justice. Process control refers to control over the dispute-resolution process and may involve opportunities of presenting input information or selecting the decision maker. Decision control refers to control over the final decision and may involve opportunities of appealing against a final verdict.

Various legal procedures of dispute resolution (e.g., arbitration, mediation, bargaining, autocratic or moot procedures) differ in the extent of such controls that either the disputant or the intervening party (i.e., the judge) may have over the resolution process. Their work has shown that compared to a "no-process- control" condition, when disputants have control over the process, they would perceive the final decision (the verdict) as fairer. Similar findings were observed in other studies in legal settings (e.g., LaTour, 1978; Lind et. al., 1980). The importance of process control in justice perceptions has received further support from research into the conflict-resolution processes in organizational settings (e.g., Sheppard, 1984; Folger & Greenberg, 1985; Greenberg & Folger, 1983) as well as between individual friends (e.g., Senchak & Reis, 1988).

The most significant advance in the concept of procedural justice can be found in Lind and Tyler's (1988) book titled "The Social Psychology of Procedural Justice". Based on empirical evidence from the legal, political, economical, organizational as well as social psychological arenas, Lind and Tyler concluded that people are more concerned with the justice of procedures than the justice of final outcomes, and that perceptions of the fairness of procedures are important determinants of attitude and behaviour. Addressing the fundamental issue of the underlying psychological reasons for the observed importance accorded procedural justice, Lind and Tyler (1988) have proposed two explanatory models. The extended self-interest model contends that concerns about procedural justice are primarily due to individuals' self-interest from a long-term perspective. Individuals aim to optimize their final outcomes by ways of process controls. An alternative explanation takes a group perspective. The group value model asserts that procedures represent norms and values of the group. Because individuals are social beings, they place high value on social interactions and group membership, they therefore have basic concerns about procedural justice.

As Lane (1988a) points out, that a third reason for a greater concern for procedural rather than outcome justice can be found in Juster and Courants (1986) notion of "process-benefits". Based on the observation that individuals derive greater satisfaction from " performing" certain activities than from the final outcome of the activities, Lane argued that people would care more for the procedures leading to a just outcome than the outcome itself.

Alongside theory development, there has been an upsurge in empirical research into procedural justice. Procedural justice research has been extended from Thibaut and Walker's pioneer work on issues related to legal dispute resolutions (for a review, see Lind & Tyler, 1988) to areas including conflict management in organizations (e.g., Chusmir & Mills, 1989; Karambayya & Brett, 1989), grievance systems (e.g., Klaas, 1989), participation and organizational democracy (e.g., Whiddon & Martin, 1989), resources allocation and recruitment (Bies & Shapiro, 1988), performance prediction (e.g., Konovsky & Cropanzano, 1991), pay raise and compensation (Folger & Konovsky, 1989), satisfaction with union

11

and management (e.g., Fryxell & Gordon, 1989), managerial promotion practice (McEnrue, 1989), as well as emplyees' reactions to layoff decisions (e.g., Brockner, 1990; Brockner et al., 1990; Konovsky & Folger, 1991).

While Lind and Tyler are more concerned with conceptual issues of procedural justice, other theorists focus on identifying the key principles of fair procedures. Leventhal, Karuza and Fry's (1980) allocation preference theory adopts such a proactive orientation. The allocation preference theory identifies several key principles that can be used to achieve justice in the allocations of resources: procedures that ensure the application of consistency rules, procedures that allow the choice of decision-making agents and the presentation of input information, procedures that safeguards against biases, procedures that observe moral and ethical standards and procedures that allow provisions for appeals against the final decision.

Empirical research generated by the allocation preference theory has also covered a variety of organizational behavior domains including resources allocations (e.g., Barrett-Howard & Tyler, 1986; Fry & Cheney, 1981; Fry & Leventhal, 1979; Sheppard & Lewicki, 1984), performance appraisal (Greenberg, 1986a, 1986b; Kanfer, Sawyer, Earley & Lind, 1987; Landy, Barnes & Murphy, 1978; Landy, Barnes-Farrel & Cleveland, 1980), as well as other managerial practices such as motivating and planning actions (Sheppard & Lewicki, 1987). These studies have provided convergent results showing that the procedures identified in the allocation preference theory are the key determinants of perceived fairness.

Interactional Justice

As a special case of procedural justice, the concept of interactional justice has recently been proposed (e.g., Bies & Moag, 1986; Lind & Tyler, 1988). Interactional justice refers to the quality of interpersonal treatment an individual receives in the process of allocation of resources. The importance of interactional justice lies in its potential in sustaining human dignity and enhancing self-esteem (Lind & Tyler, 1988). In other words, being treated fairly in social interactions and communications provides individuals with the opportunity to "experience their own dignity" (Lane, 1988a, p.316). Folger (1988) also conceptualises justice as dignity and argues that it is an intrinsic human desire to treat others and to be treated by others in a just and fair manner.

12

Research on interactional justice has focused primarily on the identification of the key criteria for fair interactions or treatments in a variety of organizational settings. The criteria identified include "open and honest communications" in recruiter-candidate interactions (Bies, 1986); "sincerity" (Bies, 1987b), "providing vital information and discussing expectations", "not harming people" (Sheppard & Lewicki, 1987), and "not bullying people" (Karambayya & Brett, 1989) in manager-subordinate interactions; "politeness and respect" in citizen-authorities interactions; as well as "seriousness of treatment" in entrepreneur-bank personnel interactions (Koper & Vermunt, 1988). Several recent research further showed that managerial behavior, indicative of interpersonal sensitivity in interactions with employees, had a "fairness-enhancing effect" on employees' perceptions of the decision making processes (e.g., Brockner, 1990; Greenberg, 1990b; Tyler & Bies, 1990). Recently, Greenberg (1990a) pointed out the need to integrate and unify these diverse yet similar phenomena in order to avoid the confusion of "conceptual overlap" (p.425).

Other Developments in Organizational Justice Research

Provisions of Justifications

One recent line of justice research focuses on "victim's desire" in seeking causal explanations for the injustice. Bies (1987a, p.304) has conceptualised perceptions of justice as the product of a process of argumentation or persuasion. Specifically, perceptions of justice or injustice of an outcome are influenced more by the provision of a social account (or explanatory justifications) for the outcome, rather than solely by the favorability of the final outcome. Bies argued that feelings of discontent or perceptions of injustice associated with unfavorable outcomes are primarily due to the inadequacy or absence of justifications, when adequate justifications are provided, feelings of injustice would be significantly reduced. Recent empirical evidence has shown that the provision of such justifications help reduce victim's feelings of injustice in workplace layoff situations (Brockner, 1990), pay cuts decisions (Greenberg, 1990b), and in interpersonal interactions between management and employees (Folger & Bies, 1989; Tyler & Bies, 1990).

Fabrications of Justice

Instead of taking the perspective of the recipient of a distribution,

13

another recent line of justice research takes a "distributor's" perspective and concentrates on " harmdoer's" (those responsible for the injustice) behaviour aiming at the maintenance of injustice. Cohen's work on "fabrications of justice" (Cohen, 1989) is representative of this new research direction. Cohen (1989) argued that harmdoers who unjustly benefit from an injustice, typically want to maintain the injustice. Their strategies may involve the creation of fabrications of justice or "false beliefs about justice". Victims of an injustice are intentionally led to hold such false beliefs and consequently, through such intentionally-induced fabrications or deceit, injustice is maintained. Cohen further argued that "voice procedures" (e.g., Lind et al., 1990; Tyler et al., 1985) could potentially be deployed to create a false belief of having control and dignity. While genuine opportunities of being able to express one's opinions typically enhance the person's fairness perception of the decision as well as his/her compliance with the goals of the decision (for a review, see Lind & Tyler, 1988), the potential deceptive use of voice procedures by harmdoers could create illusions of control and dignity in victims and thereby help the maintenance of the injustice. Cohen warned such deceptive use of voice procedures and advocated a reexamination of previous voice research "with an eye toward discovering the potentially deceptive use of the symbols of justice" (p.38).

Scope of Justice

Implicit to distributive and procedural justice theories, the scope of concern for justice is thought to be confined by group membership status. That is, concern for justice is only applicable to members of a group having mutual cooperative relations (Deutsch, 1985; Messe, Hymes, & MacCoun, 1984; Optow, 1987,1988; Tyler & Lind, 1990). In examining the effect of group membership on concern for justice, Tyler and Lind (1990) made the distinction between inclusionary effects involving the relationship among in-group members and exclusionary effects concerning the relationship among out-group members. Their data on inclusionary effects showed that centrality of group membership had an effect on justice concerns. Members of intermediate group status had the greatest concern for justice. Brockner (1990) examined the effect of layoffs in workplace on survivors' job attitudes and behavior. The results showed that when layoff victims were within the survivors' scope of justice as defined by the closeness of personal relationship or similarity in attitudes, survivors were more withdrawn from their jobs and

14

perceived that the layoffs were handled unfairly.

While most justice theories assumes that concern for justice is constraint by the scope of group boundaries (Tyler & Lind, 1990), Lerner (1982) contends that concern for justice is a basic human motive. Folger (1988) also shares a similar belief in that justice concerns are an intrinsic aspect of human behavior. Within these conceptual frameworks, an individual's concern for justice has no bound, that is, it extends to all other human beings.

The Psychology of Improving Justice

Cook (1990) has advocated a psychology of improving justice by promoting respect and liking for subordinate social groups or victims of social injustice, with the goal of extending the scope of justice to include these groups. Based on the extensive social psychological research on intergroup relations and attitude vs. value changes, Cook (1990) suggests various ways of achieving the goal. These include modifying attitudes towards subordinate groups, strengthening the values attached to justice principles, displaying behavior consistent with justice principles, employing situational influences such as legislations, and increasing the effectiveness of opposition by victims of social injustice. With reference to affirmative action policies, it has independently been argued that effective affirmative action programmes can help achieve true equality of opportunity and hence improve overall social justice (Crosby & Clayton, 1990; Pettigrew & Martin, 1987).

15

3 Literature on selection fairness

In personnel selection, the issue of selection fairness has been the main focus of the empirical literature. This literature however is dominated by two largely independent components; One concerns selection fairness with reference to the use of employment tests, and the other addresses selection fairness with regard to selection interviews (Footnotes 1 and 2).

Selection Fairness in Test Use

Although the test fairness literature has spanned three decades, some key psychometric issues are still not completely resolved. Since test fairness has been examined chiefly from the perspective of minority discrimination and affirmative action legislations, an understanding of relevant legislations on discrimination in selection becomes necessary for a review of the test fairness literature.

In a recent review, Sharf (1988) has identified the years 1964, 1971 and 1988 as "significant milestones" for the development of the definition of selection fairness. In 1964, selection fairness was clearly defined in Title VII of the Civil Rights Act. The Act reads "It shall be an unlawful employment practice for an employer: (1) to fail or refuse to hire or to discharge any individual, or otherwise to discriminate against any individual with respect to his compensation, terms, conditions or privileges of employment because of such individual's race, color, religion, sex or national origin; or (2) to limit. segregate, or classify his employees or applicants for employment in any way which would deprive or tend to deprive any individual of employment opportunities or to

16

otherwise adversely affect his status as an employee, because of such individual's race, color, religion, sex or national origin." (Title VII of the Civil Rights Act of 1964).

The emphasis of this legislation was on the rights of any individual candidate irrespective of his/her personal characteristics. The implicit implication in terms of the definition of selection fairness is that fair selections involve the use of objective job-relevant qualifications as selection criteria and hence obey the fundamental principle of meritocracy. The primary intention of Title VII was then to "eradicate any discriminatory barriers to employment opportunities" (Bolick, 1988, p.320). In the context of this legislation, discrimination is defined only in terms of differential or disparate treatment given to two similarly qualified candidates of different (racial) background.

However, the supreme court's decision in the Griggs v. Duke Power case (1971) gave an alternative interpretation to Title VII of the Civil Rights Act. Discrimination was redefined in terms of the presence of "adverse impact", that is, a lower hiring rate of minority candidates. In this context, fairness of a selection practice is determined in terms of whether it has achieved approximately equal hiring rates for both majority and minority groups. Because an objective merit-based selection would typically yield extremely low subgroup selection ratios (i.e., 6/100 or 17/100) (see Schmitt & Noe, 1986 for a review), the 1978 Uniform Guidelines on Employee Selection Procedures formally prescribed a 4/5 rule for a fair selection practice. Specifically, the 4/5 rule stipulates that the ratio of the proportion of minority candidates hired to majority candidates hired should not be lower than 4/5 (Uniform Guidelines on Employee Selection Procedures, 1978). The fundamental principle underlying selection fairness has therefore shifted from that of individual meritocracy to one stressing group equality in terms of employment results (e.g., Sharf, 1988; Gottfredson, 1988).

This definition of selection fairness in terms of group equality in selection results has prompted an upsurge of research in test validation as well as the development of "test fairness models" during the 1970s and the most part of the 1980s.

Research on Test Validation

As is originally presumed in Title VII of the Civil Rights Act of 1964, a fair selection is merit based. However, the application of the meritocracy principle in selection has had always resulted in adverse impact or a significantly lower hiring rate for minorities.

17

Because of the public's concern for the underrepresentation of minorities in the workforce and frequent legal charges against discrimination in employment selections (Footnote 3), the use of test in evaluating candidates came under serious attack. Doubts were expressed about the validity of mental tests in predicting job performance (e.g., Kirkpatrick, Ewen, Barrett & Katzell, 1968). Specifically, the public was suspicious that (1) test consistently and unfairly underpredicted minority candidates and that (2) tests can only or at best predict performance for specific jobs and under specific circumstances, and thereby their usefulness in employment selection in general is questionable. The first problem concerns issues of differential validity, and the second, issues of validity generalization. The intention to clarify these issues of test validation has led researchers to a two-decade-long research into the psychometric properties of tests.

Differential Validity

Two hypotheses about differential validity were advanced: the single-group validity hypothesis and the differential validity hypothesis. The former contends that tests may have only one validity in that they may be valid in predicting job performance of majority candidates but invalid for minority candidates. The latter holds that tests are valid predictors for both minority and majority groups but are more valid in predicting majority candidates' performance.

Results based on large scaled meta-analyses to date have rejected both the single-group validity hypothesis (e.g., Boehm, 1977; Katzell & Dyer, 1977; Linn, 1978; O'Connor, Wexley & Alexander, 1975; Schmidt, Berner & Hunter, 1973). and the differential validity hypothesis (e.g., Bartlett, Bobko, Mosier & Hannan, 1978; Hunter, Schmidt, & Hunter, 1979: Linn, 1978; Schmidt, Pearlman, & Hunter, 1980). In conclusion, Schmidt (1988) argued that employment tests are equally valid for all racial groups (p.275).

Validity Generalization

There were two theories of validity generalization. The situation-specific validity hypothesis holds that employment tests are valid only for certain situations, test validities are not generalizable across situations nor organizations. The job-specific validity hypothesis holds that tests may be valid for certain jobs and hence test validities are not generalizable across jobs. Results to date have also rejected both the situation-specific hypothesis (e.g., Callendar & Osburn, 1980; Schmidt, Hunter, Pearlman & Hirsh, 1985; Raju & Burke, 1983) and the job-specific hypothesis (e.g., Hunter, 1980; Schmidt, Hunter & Pearlman, 1981). Schmidt (1988) recently concluded that employment tests, in particular cognitive ability tests, are valid predictors of most jobs under varied settings and situations.

Research on the Development of Test Fairness Models

As much as the concern for the predictive validity of employment tests, the American public was equally concerned about how these tests were used in the evaluation of candidates. Specifically, the procedures of choosing cut-off points and of applying the test-regression lines.

The selection procedures based on the meritocracy principle are represented by the Cleary model of test fairness (Cleary, 1968). The model holds that if the test-criterion relationships are different for the minority and majority groups, then the use of separate regression lines for each subgroup in predicting job performance would eliminate either an under- or over- prediction of the performance of any particular group. The selection procedures prescribed in the Cleary (1968) model were since adopted by the Equal Employment Opportunity Commission's Uniform Guidelines on Employee Selection Procedures (1978).

However, as mentioned earlier, selection procedures that are merit-based almost always result in adverse impact (i.e., lower hiring rate of minorities). Because of the societal and ethical concern about reducing such adverse impact, researchers focused on the development of alternative procedures or models aiming at eliminating differential rates of subgroup hiring.

Darlington's (1971) subjective regression model involves the setting of different performance criteria for different subgroups (typically a lower performance criterion for the minority subgroup). This selection procedure thus involves the lowering of job performance criterion for the minorities and thereby increases the hiring rate for minority candidates.

Einhorn and Bass's (1971) equal risk model involves the specification of a minimal pass score for the performance criteria (e.g., 70%). The predictor cut-off scores corresponding to the specified criteria are then determined separately for the subgroups. Because the same criterion cut-off is used for all subgroups, both majority and minority candidates so selected would have a similar expected chance of success (or failure) on the job.

Coles's (1973) threshold utility model also involves the specification of a minimal satisfactory criterion score. However, this model further stipulates that above this criterion cut-off, the probability of being selected for the minority candidates should be the same as that for the majority candidates.

Thorndike's (1971) constant ratio model also involves the specification of a minimal satisfactory cut-off point on the criterion measure. The model further requires that above this criterion cut-off, the proportion of candidate selection ratio between the subgroups should be equal to the success ratio between the subgroups.

In critical analyses of these test fairness models (Hunter & Schmidt, 1976;Jenkins, 1980; Peterson & Novick, 1976; Schmidt & Hunter, 1974), it was concluded that "the most easily applied and rationally consistent model is Cleary's approach" (Schmitt & Noe, 1986; p.93) and that all the other alternative models using minimal performance criterion are essentially procedures of "producing disguised quota hiring systems" (Schmidt, 1988; p.282).

However, the most important conclusion derived from these analyses is that almost none of the selection procedures proposed in these models would succeed in what they purport to achieve, that is, to eliminate adverse impact, they merely reduce the discrepancy in hiring rates between majority and minority groups (e.g., Schmidt, 1988; p.288). Furthermore, utility research has shown that a small reduction in adverse impact typically is at the expense of significant losses in overall estimated organizational productivity (e.g., Schmitt & Noe, 1986). Therefore, the goal of achieving equality in subgroup selection rates (i.e., to eliminate adverse impact) on the one hand, and the goal of optimising organizational productivity, on the other hand, appear to be virtually incompatible. Given the immense legal and societal pressures on subgroup equality in selection rates, researchers have turned to utility analyses in search for the best balanced "tradeoff" between the two goals. Selection fairness research has over the years turned from considerations of validity to those of the utility of selection procedures. Fairness issues are thus reduced to a question of utility (Cascio, 1987, 1991).

Utility Analyses in the Pursuit of Identifying the Best "Tradeoff""

Utility analysis has been used to estimate in dollar terms the net gains in using a predictor (test) in selection over and above the "base rate", that is, the % of successful selection without the use of the predictor. The idea of applying utility analysis to the tradeoff problem between selection equality and productivity, originally came from Hunter, Schmidt and Rauschenberger (1977). In the context of this tradeoff problem in selection, utility analyses take into account not only the psychometric properties of a selection procedure, but also the psychological, social, ethical and legal consequences of the procedure (e.g., Cascio, 1991; Hunter & Schmidt, 1976; Petersen & Novick, 1976). In the examination of the costs and benefits of a selection procedure, utility analyses consider both objective costs including those of job turnover and proficiency, and subjective costs such as psychological and social costs of job failure and false rejections. Although Hartigan and Wigdor (1989) argued that "the current state of economic knowledge does not permit estimation of the overall economic effects of widespread testing" (p.248), utility analyses are nonetheless still regarded by many (e.g., Schmidt et al., 1992) as the most suitable and valid method in the identification of the best tradeoff between equality and productivity.

Schmidt, Mack and Hunter (1984) directly compared the relative utility gains among three selection procedures: the Cleary procedure (i.e., merit-based or complete top-down method) and two quota hiring selection procedures. The quota procedures involved the use of minimal predictor cut-off scores; one method used the mean of the predictor score as the cut-off, the other set the predictor cut-off at the point equivalent to one standard deviation below the mean. As compared to the productivity gain of the complete top-down method (the Cleary method), lowering the predictor cut-off to the mean score resulted in a relative net gain of 45% (or a loss of 55%), lowering the predictor cut-off further down to 1 SD below the mean yielded a relative net gain of 16% (or loss of 84%). The use of minimal performance criteria thus results in significant loss in productivity terms.

Using such utility comparisons, the best tradeoff selection procedures identified so far involve a "top-down within subgroup" selection method. This method employs the top-down selection procedure for each subgroup separately and therefore results in the selection of the best qualified candidates from within each subgroup. It has been shown that among all quota hiring systems, this within-group top-down method, not only completely eliminates adverse impact (Schmidt, 1988; p.288), but also yields the least productivity loss (5% to 15% as compared to the Cleary method) than any of the other quota methods (e.g., Cronbach &

21

Schaeffer, 1981; Cronbach, Yalow & Schaeffer, 1980; Hunter & Hunter, 1984; Hunter et al, 1977; Schmidt et al, 1984). Several researchers (e.g., Hartigan & Wigdor, 1989; McKinney, 1987; Schmidt, 1988; Wigdor & Hartigan, 1988) recently conclude that it is difficult to identify an alternative selection method that represents a better tradeoff between the goals of optimising productivity and eliminating adverse impact.

However, despite its current popularity, this top-down within-group selection method is also regarded as discriminatory because a job-irrelevant factor, candidate ethnicity, is used explicitly as a hiring criterion (e.g., Lerner, 1977, 1979; Schmitt & Robertson, 1990, p.309). It now appears that in order to eliminate adverse impact, a non-job relevant hiring criterion would have to be used. In other words, selections based solely on merits would always result in adverse impact. The reason for this lies in the existence of significant subgroup differences in job-relevant abilities, specifically in general cognitive abilities or the "g" (general intelligence) factor.

Evidence on Subgroup Differences in Job-Relevant Abilities

There has been cummulative and consistent evidence showing that cognitive ability and special aptitude tests are among the most valid predictors of job performance. Hunter (1980, 1986) found that the predictive relevance of cognitive ability increases as the level of job complexity increases. Hunter and Hunter's (1984) meta-analysis revealed an average predictive validity of .49 of the general cognitive ability (based on the General Aptitude Test Battery) in predicting job performance. It has been claimed that cognitive ability tests can make better overall performance predictions than any other known predictors (Gottfredson, 1988, p.295).

The reason for the superior performance predictability of cognitive ability tests lies in two facts: First, according to job analysis data, the very fundamental performance requirements of almost all jobs can be represented by Spearman's "g" factor (e.g., Arvey, 1986; Gottfredson, 1986a, 1986b), and second, all cognitive ability tests basically measure this "g" factor (e.g., Thorndike, 1986; Gottfredson & Crouse, 1986). The g or general intelligence factor represents the underlying general capacity for abstract thinking, reasoning and problem solving skills (e.g., Snyderman & Rothman, 1986). There is evidence that the g factor is genetically linked (e.g., Jensen, 1986) and that the concept of g is reflected in the notion of "multiple intelligence" (Gardner, 1983; White, 1988) as well as the notion of "practical intelligence" (Peters, 1987).

Turning back to the dilemma between the use of objective or merit-based selection criteria and the elimination of adverse impact, it is because of the existence of significant subgroup differences in "g" that this dilemma remains unsolved. Evidence on the differences in g between racial subgroups has been well documented and reviewed (for reviews, see Eysenck, 1984; Gottfredson, 1986b; Jensen, 1981, 1985; Schmitt & Noe, 1986; Wigdor & Garner, 1982). The size of such subgroup ability difference appears to be around one standard deviation (Schmitt, 1989).

A Return to Objective Merit-Based Definition of Selection Fairness

The implications of such differences are clear for the fairness of selection outcomes: So long as subgroup ability differences exist, it is theoretically difficult to define fairness of a selection in terms of the absence of adverse impact. This is because the absence of adverse impact means equal rates of selection for subgroups which in turn carries the presumption that subgroups are equally merited in terms of job-relevant qualifications. Consequently, a call for the return of the original definition for selection fairness based on meritocracy has been voiced recently (e.g., Gottfredson, 1988; Sharf, 1988).

Amidst this climate of reconsidering selection fairness in terms of objective merits among academics, the Supreme Court decision in the "Watson v. Fort Worth Bank and Trust" case in 1988 further marked the legal support for the returning to objective employment criteria. In its decision in the Waston case, the Court expressed willingness to reconsider and to clarify its earlier selection fairness definition, used in the 1971 Griggs case, in terms of the absence of adverse impact. From a legislative perspective, the 1988 Court decision thus allow employers to "refocus on individual merit as the touchstone of equal employment opportunity" (Sharf, 1988; p.236).

The trend continues in the 1989 Supreme Court decision in the Ward Cove Packing Co. v. Antonio case. The Supreme Court ruling has further placed the responsibility to prove discrimination on racial grounds on the part of complaining employees and the prosecuting lawyers. In such cases, the employers accused are no longer required to "bear the burden of proof", that is, to prove "business necessity" in order to justify their selection practices which have an adverse impact on minorities.

While research effort to date has clarified the psychometric, utility and differential ability issues relating to quota-based vs. merit-based selections, the rights and wrongs of such selections are still being intensely debated at all sectors of the society. With the psychometric debates over validation and fairness models abating (Guion & Gibson, 1988) and evidence on the existence of subgroup ability differences becoming increasingly conclusive, selection fairness research is now reassuming its original focus on ethical and social justice concerns.

✓ *Selection Fairness in Employment Interviews*

Unlike the test fairness literature whereby early studies revealed differential test validities for minority and majority candidates (e.g., Kirkpatrick et al, 1968), early validation studies of selection interviews simply failed to agree on the more fundamental question of whether in the first place, the interview is a valid predictor of job performance (e.g., Lopez, 1966; Kirkpatrick et al, 1968). This question is still the focus of several research to date.

Using meta-analysis, Hunter and Hunter (1984) reported an average validity of .09 for interviews. However, subsequent research showed that interview validity may have been underestimated. For instance, Wiesner and Cronshaw (1988) found that after corrections for statistical artifacts including range restriction and criteria unreliability, interviews in general have a mean validity of .47. The development of systematically constructed "structured interviews" further improved the predictive validity of interviews (e.g., Arvey, Miller, Gould & Burch, 1987; Cronshaw & Wiesner, 1989; Pursell, Campion & Gaylord, 1980; Wiesner & Cronshaw, 1988).

Recently two special forms of structured interviews have been developed. In situational interviews (Latham, Saari, Pursell & Campion, 1980) whereby candidates are required to indicate how they would behave in given job situations identified by the critical incidents method. The predictive validity of situational interviews has been around .30 and .46 (e.g., Campion, Pursell & Brown,1988; Latham & Saari, 1984; Latham et al, 1980; Weekley & Gier, 1987). In addition, greater interviewer agreement has been found in situational interviews than in traditional structured interviews (Maurer & Fay, 1988).

The other form of structured interview is the patterned behavioral description interview (PBDI) (Janz, 1982,1987,1988; Janz, Hellervik & Gillmore, 1986). The questions asked in the PBDI is also based on the analysis of critical incidents. However, instead of

24

asking candidates to indicate how they would react in such incidents as in the situational interviews, the PBDI asks the candidate to recall from his/her recent past, an incident similar to the situation described in one of the critical incidents and to describe how he/she reacted on that occasion. The range of predictive validity for PBDI has been around .45 and .72 (Janz, 1989). Interviews, if properly constructed, can therefore be a valid predictor of job performance.

Fairness of Interview Evaluations

In the context of selection fairness, one key question concerns whether interviews differentially predict minority and majority candidates. There has been only limited research on this issue of interview differential validity. Based on traditional unstructured interviews, Freytag (1976) found that the interview is equally valid for subgroups. Since then, there has been three validation studies using "situational interviews", the conclusion is that situational interviews equally predict male and female candidates but slightly over-predicted minority performance (Arvey et al, 1987; Campion eta al, 1988; Latham et al, 1980).

So, like tests, when interviews are used as a predictor of job performance, equally valid predictions (or at least no underpredictions for minorities) can be made about candidates from different subgroups. However, unlike tests which are typically objective measures of candidates' covert, implicit and sometimes innate capacities (e.g., the g factor), interviews represent a more subjective means of assessing their overt, explicit and observable behaviour. Beause of this element of subjectivity in candidate evaluation in interviews, fairness considerations of interviews would have to address an additional question of whether subgroup candidates who are equally merited, (on other independent objective measures such as qualifications and experience), would be given different interview evaluations.

Indeed the bulk of the selection interview literature has been devoted to this issue of unfair discrimination in terms of differential evaluations based on job-irrelevant factors such as applicants' sex, age, or race. There have been three reviews of relevant studies to date (Arvey, 1979; Arvey & Campion, 1982; Campion & Arvey, 1989).

25

Gender Bias Effect

Although Arvey's (1979) early review suggested that interviewers may be biased against women, several later studies found no evidence of a gender bias effect in interview evaluations (e.g., Graves & Powell, 1988; McDonald & Hakel, 1985). However, recent research trend has shifted from this "all-or-none" approach to one that emphasizing the identification of contextual or situational variables that are inducive of a gender bias effect. Three contextual variables have been identified by Campion and Arvey (1989). The first concerns the composition of the total applicant pool. Heilman (1980) showed that when females represent a larger proportion of the original applicant pool, the gender bias effect was reduced significantly. The second contextual variable relates to the type of the job. In a meta-analysis of 19 studies using "male-type" jobs (Olian, Shwarb & Haberfeld, 1988) found only "marginal" (p.180) evidence of a gender bias effect. In contrast, a reversed gender bias effect, in favour of females candidates, was found in studies of "female-type" jobs (e.g., Arvey et al, 1987; Parsons & Liden, 1984). The third contextual variable concerns the adequacy of available job-relevant information about the candidates. Campion and Arvey's (1989) conclusion was that when more adequate job-relevant information is available to interviewers, gender bias effects tend to diminish (e.g., Powell, 1987; Tosi & Einbender, 1985). However, in a well-designed study not included in Campion and Arvey's review (1989), it has been shown that gender bias effect still exist when a great deal of job-relevant information is provided to the interviewers (Hitt & Barr, 1989).

Another contextual variable, not mentioned in Campion and Arvey's (1989) review, concerns the provision of information about successful woman professionals to interviewers prior to selection interviews. Heilman and Martell (1986) found that repeated exposure to relevant and representative information about a group of successful women could help eliminate gender bias effect in interviewers' decision making.

Age Bias Effect

Earlier studies in the 1970s typically showed an age bias effect (e.g., Haefner, 1977). Evidence based on post 1980 studies suggests that the age bias effect may be influenced by either contextual variables or the research design used. In terms of contextual variables, studies showed that the extent of the age bias effect could be

26

enhanced by making interviewers feel accountable for their decisions (Gordon, 1984). The effect could however be eliminated under a "low accountability" condition (Gordon, Rozelle & Baxter, 1989). In addition, it was found that age bias effect diminished when the original applicant pool is composed of a larger proportion of older candidates (Cleveland, Festa & Montgomery, 1988).

The research design used also moderates the age bias effect in interview decisions; typically an age bias effect was observed in studies using a resume design (Young & Allison, 1982; Young & Voss, 1986), but not in studies using an interview design (Young & Ponder, 1985; Ponder, 1987; Hitt & Barr, 1989).

Ethnicity Effect

Evidence based on laboratory simulated interview studies so far has revealed either no significant ethnicity effect (Arvey, 1979; McDonald & Hakel, 1985), or a reversed ethnicity effect whereby black candidates received more favourable interview evaluations (Mullins, 1982).

In a field study involving actual interviews, Parsons and Liden (1984) showed that blacks candidates were given lower interview ratings. However, as Campion and Arvey (1989, p. 69) pointed out that, unlike laboratory studies, under actual interview conditions there was no control over the job-relevant qualifications of minority and majority candidates. Despite this, the recent laboratory study by Hitt & Barr (1989) also showed a significant ethnicity effect in managers' interview decisions.

At the conclusion of the latest review on unfair discrimination in employment interview, Campion and Arvey (1989) confessed that there is still insufficient evidence on the issue to draw firm conclusions (p.70). Why are the interview results mixed and inconsistent, the answer in part lies in methodological considerations.

Methodological Considerations in Interview Fairness Research

Although almost the entire literature on unfair discrimination in selection interviews is experimental and laboratory-based, not all these studies observe stringently the essential criteria in the design of a good experiment. A good laboratory study typically possesses high internal and external validity (Campbell & Stanley, 1967; Cook & Campbell, 1976). In the context of employment interview research, major considerations of internal validity involve the need for manipulation checks and the control for demand characteristics (Kacmar, Tatcliff & Ferris, 1989). Manipulation checks help to ensure that (a) experimental treatments or manipulations are perceived by subjects in a similar manner as they are intended by the experimenter, and (b) other potential confounding variables are held constant across experimental treatment conditions. These in turn help to ensure that observed variations in dependent measures are only due to variations in the independent treatments. Presence of demand characteristics may serve as a cue to subjects in terms of desired responses or experimenter expectations (Fisher, 1984). Control for such demand characteristics helps to ensure that results are not biased because subjects consciously try to conform to what they see as expected of them.

Major considerations of external validity of interview fairness research involve the choice of information type (i.e., resume vs. interview) as well as subject sample (i.e., students vs. professionals). Ample research has been carried out to examine the generalizability of interview findings from resume-based to interview-based studies (e.g., Singer, 1988) and from studies using student subjects to those using manager subjects (Locke, 1986; Singer & Sewell, 1989; Singer & Bruhns, 1991).

In the interview literature, studies have varied significantly in terms of the controls over threats to both internal and external validities. Because of these methodological differences, it is virtually impossible to draw firm or valid conclusions about the various discriminatory effects. As interview researchers become more concerned with these methodological issues and hence interview research are more stringently designed, consistent and valid results may then be obtained with reference to applicant bias effects. For instance, one recent study (Hitt & Barr, 1989) is considered as the most rigorous in interview research (Kacmar, Ratcliff & Ferris, 1989, p.37; Morrow, Mullen & McElroy, 1990, p.142) because the study has (a) provided controls for demand characteristics, (b) conducted manipulation checks, (c) used a videotaped simulation of interviews and (d) used professional manager subjects. Hitt and Barr's results revealed both a sex bias and an ethnicity bias effect in managers' interview decisions. However, no age bias effect was evident in managers' candidate evaluations.

Conclusions

From the general introduction in Chapter one, it becomes clear that the fairness of an organization's selection practice is of significant importance to all potential job candidates as well as to the organization. The literature on current organizational justice theories suggests that these theories provide a comprehensive and integrative conceptual framework for research into fairness issues in organizations. The present review of the selection fairness literature has revealed that fairness research in personnel selection has to date focused on discriminatory issues related to the use of tests and interviews. While research into test fairness has focused on psychometric, validation and utility issues, interview fairness research has concentrated on the identification of sources of bias in interview decision making. No systematic application of the organizational justice conceptual framework has yet been made to selection fairness research. Such an approach would shift the focus of selection fairness research from psychometric and bias issues to one of social justice concern. The approach would further enhance understanding of fairness issues in selection from the perspectives of outcome justice, procedural justice and other current justice notions. The following chapters identify areas in selection research to which organizational justice theories could be fruitfully applied. The chapters also report the limited available research that has taken such an approach.

Footnote 1   Almost the entire empirical literature on selection fairness is based on studies carried out in the United States. This is because the American society and legal political bodies have pressed for the consideration of this issue since the 1960s. Similar literature from other countries such as the United Kingdom, Australia, Canada and New Zealand is either of insignificant quantity or virtually non-existent. Schmitt and Noe (1986, p.72) concluded that "it is likely an examination of selection procedures in other multicultural societies would yield evidence of a similar (kind)". Indeed, the two U.K. studies on the utility of various selection methods (Pearn, 1989; Smith, 1989) reported similar standard deviations of performance in Great Britain to those found in the States (Schmidt & Hunter, 1983).

Footnote 2   The literature on selection fairness with reference to other predictors such as assessment centers and work sample tests is much limited in volume. Interested readers are referred to Cascio (1987, 1991) or Schmitt & Noe (1986).

Footnote 3   One recurrent point of the chapter concerns the "legal or societal pressure for subgroup equality in employment opportunities".   The ethical, philosophical and psychological justifications for the demand are reviewed in Chapter 5 in the context of preferential selection).

4 Applying procedural justice notions to selection research

There are two areas in selection research to which procedural justice notions could be applied. The first concerns the identification of fairness determinants of selection procedures; the second concerns possible consequences of candidates' fairness perceptions about selection procedures. The rationales and relevant research findings are reviewed as follows.

Identification of Determinants of Fair Selection Procedures

The three studies to be reported in this chapter address the general question of what makes a selection practice fair. More specifically, the question asks what are the key features of selection procedures that are considered fair. The studies aim to identify directly the underlying determinants of a fair selection practice. Leventhal et al.'s (1980) allocation preference theory provides an integrative conceptual framework for such a research question. The allocation preference theory proposes six general principles that represent the key features of fair procedures in situations involving resources allocations. These principles are: consistency in applying rules, bias avoidance, accuracy of information, correctability of decisions, choice of decision makers, and ethicality. The theory has generated a great deal of research into procedural justice in organizational settings (see chapter one for a review). Research findings are in general supportive of the theory. For instance, Greenberg (1986a) examined the determinants of fair performance appraisal systems.

The study used an open-ended question in gathering statements of fair performance appraisals, and the factor analysis technique in identifying the key fairness determinants. Five key determinants of fair appraisal procedures were identified in the study (soliciting input prior to evaluation and using it, two-way communication during interview, ability to challenge evaluation, rater familiarity with ratee's work, and consistent application of standards). These factors are in close agreement with the principles of procedural fairness proposed by the allocation preference theory (Greenberg, 1986a).

Using a similar method, studies 1 to 3 aim at extending Leventhal et al.'s (1980) principles of procedural fairness to personnel selection practices. Because the level or status of the position has been shown to affect both selection processes and selection decisions (e.g., Barr & Hitt, 1986; Hopper, 1977; Hopper & Williams, 1973; Kalin & Rayko, 1978; Singer & Sewell, 1989), applicants for different-level positions may have a different set of perceptions of selection fairness. Accordingly, study 1 examines fairness determinants of entry-level job selections, studies 2 and 3 concerns fairness determinants of supervisory or managerial selections. Studies 1 and 2 were conducted in New Zealand and hence were composed of NZ samples. Study 3 was carried out in Australia with an Australian sample. A similar design applies to all three studies.

Design of the Studies

The method used followed broadly that of Greenberg's (1986a) study in identifying determinants of perceived fairness of a promotion system. There were two stages in data collection. In the first stage, statements of fair determinants of a selection practice were collected and grouped. A Likert-type questionnaire based on the grouped statements was constructed. Stage 2 involved subjects completing the questionnaire by making importance ratings. These ratings were then factor-analysed for the identification of key factors of perceived fairness in selections.

Subjects and Procedures of Study 1 (Entry-Level Selection)

Altogether 290 subjects took part in Study 1. There were 166 (57.2%) males and 124 (42.8%) females. The age range was between 19 and 38 years with a mean of 21.09 years. All subjects were recruited from a large undergraduate course in business administration at the University of Canterbury. All had applied for at least one entry level job. The number of such applications for each subject ranged between 1 to 13 with a mode of 2. Positions sought included shop attendant, supermarket cashier, filing clerk, motel cleaning positions, administrative or research assistants, sales assistant or trainee positions and all were temporary full-time jobs particularly suitable for student vacation employments.

The first stage of the study involved the generation of determinants of fair selection procedures. Subjects were asked to think of their own experiences in job applications and to identify the one most important factor that would make the selection fair. Altogether 89 non-repeated statements were collected and sorted out independently by two researchers into similar groupings of determinants. Of these, 78 statements were grouped identically. The other 11 statements were then analysed and regrouped. Thus there was an 87.5% inter-judge agreement. As a result, the original 89 statements were reduced to 21 determinants of fairness in selection. These 21 statements were used to construct a Likert-type questionnaire for use in stage two of data collection.

The second stage of the study consisted of importance ratings. Subjects were asked to rate the importance of each of the 21 statements as determinants of fair selection practices. The rating scale used was an 11-point bipolar scale ranging from "not important at all" (0) to "extremely important" (10).

Results of Study 1

The mean importance ratings for the 21 determinants were calculated and the results are presented in Table 1. A t-test for independent samples was used to compare the mean ratings of male and female subjects. Sex differences were found on 7 of the 21 determinants. All subjects' responses were then factor analysed by using the principle-factor and varimax rotation technique. Using an Eigenvalue criterion, five factors accounting for 69.9% of the total variance were identified. Factor 1 "consistency in criteria and procedures, and choice of selectors," accounted for 23.7% of the variance. Factor 2, "honest, open and thorough communication," accounted for 15.9% of the variance. Factor 3, "ethicality," accounted for 10.5% of the variance. Factor 4, "bias suppression" and Factor 5, "information soliciting," accounted for 10.2% and 9.6% of the total variance respectively. The factor loadings for each factor are presented in Table 2. The alpha coefficients for the five factors were

33

Table 1
Mean importance ratings: Study 1

Determinant	All subjects	Men	Women	t
	M (SD) importance ratings by			
1. Use of interviews in gathering information	5.61 (1.81)	5.51 (1.84)	5.74 (1.77)	
2. Advertisement of every position for open competition	7.24 (1.95)	7.02 (2.08)	7.53 (1.73)	-2.27*
3. Job-related competence as key criterion	6.86 (1.71)	7.08 (1.62)	6.56 (1.79)	2.58**
4. Avoidance of nepotism	7.51 (2.29)	7.36 (2.48)	7.71 (2.00)	
5. Group of interviewers used	5.75 (2.12)	5.52 (2.23)	6.04 (1.94)	-2.11*
6. Detailed feedback to ensure that selection was carefully carried out	6.50 (1.94)	6.49 (2.02)	6.51 (1.85)	
7. Academic qualifications as key criterion	5.58 (1.68)	5.60 (1.86)	5.56 (1.41)	
8. Chance for applicant to make a case for himself/herself in selection process	7.43 (1.68)	7.39 (1.75)	7.50 (1.58)	
9. Psychological tests in selection	4.92 (2.08)	5.05 (2.10)	4.73 (2.05)	
10. Avoidance of personality as a criterion	5.92 (2.03)	5.95 (2.07)	5.88 (1.97)	
11. Equal opportunity regardless of sex, age, or race	8.96 (1.56)	8.66 (1.74)	9.36 (1.17)	-4.09**
12. Same selection procedures for every applicant	8.48 (1.78)	8.33 (1.91)	8.68 (1.59)	
13. Clear, honest, two-way communication in interviews for applicant to get a realistic picture of job	8.28 (1.67)	8.12 (1.69)	8.48 (1.61)	
14. Personality as an important criterion	4.46 (2.20)	4.31 (2.31)	4.67 (2.02)	
15. Employer has not made a decision prior to interview	8.86 (1.61)	8.63 (1.89)	9.15 (1.08)	-2.97**
16. Equal number of male and female interviewers on panel	5.27 (2.57)	4.64 (2.49)	6.10 (2.44)	-5.02**
17. Competent interviewers	7.86 (1.83)	7.71 (1.93)	8.06 (1.69)	
18. Avoidance of looks as a criterion	7.36 (2.04)	7.08 (2.05)	7.72 (1.99)	-2.65**
19. Collection of recommendations or references in addition to application forms	6.29 (2.03)	6.16 (2.11)	6.47 (1.91)	
20. Chance to meet boss or supervisor before deciding to take the job	6.57 (2.08)	6.52 (2.15)	6.63 (1.98)	
21. Sufficient time for interviews	7.19 (1.84)	7.08 (1.97)	7.32 (1.65)	

*p < .05 (two-tailed test).   **p < .01 (two-tailed test).

34

Table 2

Factor loadings and mean importance ratings of factors in study 1

Factor and determinant	Loading for factor					M
	1	2	3	4	5	
Consistency in criteria and procedure, and Choice of Selectors						6.39
Job related competence as key criterion	.77					
Group of interviewers used	.60					
Academic qualifications as key criterion	.55					
Same selection procedures for every applicant	.69					
Equal number of male and female interviewers on panel	.55					
Honest, open and thorough communication						7.48
Detailed feedback to ensure that selection was carefully carried out		.59				
Clear, honest, two-way communication in interviews for applicant to get a realistic picture of job		.63				
Employer has not made a decision prior to interview		.50				
Chance to meet the boss or supervisor before deciding to take the job		.66				
Sufficient time for interviews		.66				
Ethicality						8.24
Avoidance of nepotism			.74			
Equal opportunity regardless of sex, age, or race			.66			
Bias Suppression						5.91
Avoidance of personality as a criterion				.67		
Personality as an important criterion				-.52		
Avoidance of looks as a criterion				.61		
Information Soliciting						5.95
Use of interviews in gathering information					.72	
Collection of recommendations or references in addition to application forms					.64	

.49, .66, .55, .44 and .43.

The mean importance ratings of the whole sample were also calculated for each of the five factors. The most important factor was Factor 3, ethicality (mean = 8.24). Factor 2, honest, open and thorough communication, was the second most important (mean = 7.48). The mean ratings for factor 1, factor 5 and factor 4 were 6.39, 5.95 and 5.91 respectively.

Subjects and Procedures of Study 2 (Managerial Selection Using a New Zealand Sample)

This research sample consisted of 81 professionals attending the 1987 National Conference of the New Zealand Association of Training and Development in Christchurch, New Zealand. There were 17 females and 64 males. At the time of testing, all subjects were professional trainers or teachers of human resources management and were holding supervisory or managerial positions in either public organizations or private consultancy firms. Each subject had applied for between 1 to 8 supervisory or managerial positions.

The same procedures used in Study 1 were followed. In the first phase of the study, subjects were asked to think of their own experiences in applying for a supervisory or managerial position and to write down the most important factors that make a selection fair. Thirty-five non-repeated statements were generated and sorted out independently by the same two researchers as in Study 1 into similar groupings of determinants. Of the 35 statements, 25 were grouped (or left as single statements) identically by the two researchers. This represents a 71.4% inter-judge agreement. As a result of further discussion, the original 35 statements were reduced to 29 determinants of selection fairness. The same sample were then asked to rate the importance of each of the 29 statements as determinants of fair selection procedures on an 11-point bipolar rating scale from "not important at all"(0) to"extremely important" (10).

Results of Study 2

The mean importance ratings are presented in Table 3. As there were only 17 females (20%) in the sample, no analysis on sex differences was performed. The results of the principle-factor analysis using the varimax rotation technique are given in Table 4.

Six factors accounting for 69.6% of the total variance were

Table 3
Mean importance ratings: Study 2

Determinant	M rating	(SD) importance
1. Impartial interviewers	6.44	(2.66)
2. Job analysis conducted to clearly identify criteria required and use of only the identified criteria in selection	7.68	(2.48)
3. Honesty of the company in discussing its weaknesses and future plans for change	7.67	(2.47)
4. Past work experience as a criterion	5.79	(2.23)
5. Careful cross-check of references and qualifications	6.79	(2.28)
6. A selection panel without the present job incumbent, allowing the applicant to freely express ideas for changes in the way the position should be handled	6.25	(3.08)
7. Use of quantified method by assigning check points to each applicant for objective comparisons	5.91	(2.21)
8. Chance to check compatibility before taking the job	6.05	(2.48)
9. Use of interviews in gathering information	7.37	(2.07)*
10. Advertisement of every position for open competition	7.37	(2.39)
11. Job-related competence as key criterion	7.01	(2.32)
12. Avoidance of nepotism	7.90	(2.42)
13. Group of interviewers used	5.43	(2.98)
14. Detailed feedback to ensure that selection was carefully carried out	7.12	(2.09)*
15. Academic qualifications as criterion	4.24	(2.12)*
16. Chance for applicant to make a case for himself/herself in the selection process	8.42	(1.63)*
17. Psychological tests in selection	4.41	(2.48)
18. Avoidance of personality as criterion in selection	6.07	(2.14)
19. Equal opportunity regardless of sex, age, or race	9.09	(1.73)
20. Same selection procedure for every applicant	8.61	(2.13)
21. Clear, honest, two-way communication in interviews for a realistic picture of job	9.35	(1.22)*
22. Importance of personality as a criterion	4.40	(2.38)
23. Employer has not made a decision before the interview	9.20	(1.60)
24. Equal number of male and female interviewers	4.30	(3.26)
25. Competent interviewers	8.78	(1.79)*
26. Avoidance of looks as a criterion	7.24	(3.01)*
27. Collection of recommendations or references in addition to application forms	7.12	(2.43)*
28. Chance to meet boss or supervisor before taking the job	8.27	(2.12)*
29. Sufficient time for interviews	9.27	(1.20)*

Asterisks indicate ratings significantly different from those by subjects in Study 1 (p < .01).

Table 4

Factor loadings and mean importance ratings of factors in study 2

Factor and determinant	Loading for factor						M
	1	2	3	4	5	6	
Honest, Open and Thorough Communication and Choice of Selectors							7.55
Impartial interviewers	.49						
Honesty of company in discussing its weaknesses and future plans for change	.63						
Detailed feedback to know selection was carefully carried out	.62						
Clear, honest, two-way communication in interviews for applicants to get a realistic picture of job	.57						
Employer has not made a decision before interview	.67						
Equal number of male and female interviewers on panel	.74						
Competent interviewers	.51						
Information Soliciting							7.04
Job analysis conducted to clearly identify criteria		.57					
A selection panel without the present job incumbent, allowing the applicant to express ideas for changes		.75					
Use of interviews in gathering information		.62					
Careful cross-check of references and qualifications		.66					
Collection of recommendations or references in addition to application forms		.66					
Open Objective Competition							6.52
Past work experience as a criterion			.68				
Use of quantified method by assigning check points for objective comparisons			.70				
Advertisement of every position for open competition			.65				
Job-related competence as a criterion			.79				
Consistency and Ethicality							8.85
Equal opportunity regardless of sex, age, or race				.66			
Same selection procedure for every applicant				.74			
Bias Avoidance							8.16
Avoidance of nepotism					.86		
Chance to let applicant make a case for himself/herself in the selection process					.52		
Prior Knowledge of Future Colleagues							7.16
Chance to meet the work group to check compatibility before taking the job						.61	
Chance to meet the boss or supervisor before taking the job						.74	

Source: Tables 1 to 4 inclusive appeared originally in *Genetic, Social and General Psychology Monographs*, 1990, 116, pp 477-494. Reprinted with permission of the Helen Dwight Reid Educational Foundation. Published by Heldref Publications, 1319 18th Street, N.W. Washington, D.C. 20036-1802. Copyright 1990.

identified. Factor 1, "honest, open and thorough communication and choice of selectors," accounted for 16.9% of the variance. Factor 2, "information soliciting," accounted for 12.9% of the variance. Factor 3, "open-objective competition based on job-relevant criteria," accounted for 11.4% of the variance, Factor 4 "consistency and ethicality"; Factor 5, "bias-avoidance and voice,"; and Factor 6, "prior knowledge of future colleagues"; each accounted for 10.7%, 9.2% and 8.5% of the total variance respectively. The alpha coefficients for the six factors were .63, .65, .49, .69, .64, and .56.

The mean importance ratings for each of the six factors were calculated. Factor 4,"consistency and ethicality," was rated as the most important (mean = 8.85.) Factor 5, "bias-avoidance" was the second most important (mean = 8.16). The mean ratings were 7.55, 7.16, 7.04 and 6.52 for Factors 1, 6, 2, and 3 respectively.

Subjects and Procedures of Study 3 (Managerial Selection Using An Australian Sample)

This study employed a postal survey technique. The research questionnaire consisted of 28 of the 29 statements used in Study 2. The covering letter contained the following information:

"I am writing to invite you to take part in a survey designed to identify the sorts of factors that are crucial in making a personnel selection practice fair. I have already carried out some preliminary work by asking a sample of professional volunteers, who have had experiences in applying for various managerial positions, to list down the most important factors (in their views) that make a selection fair. As a result, I have collected 28 such factors. I would be grateful if you would go through these factors to make judgements regarding the fairness of managerial selection practices in general. The confidentiality of your responses is strictly assured."

Respondents' importance ratings were made on an 11-point rating scale ("0": extremely unimportant", "10": extremely important).

The questionnaire was posted to a randomly selected pool of 680 male professional managers (general, marketing, production and technical managers) in public and private organizations in Australia. The Key Business Directory of Australia (1990) was used in the random sampling. Eighteen questionnaires were returned because the persons were no longer at the addresses. Altogether 233 responses were received. The response rate was 35.2%. Of these, five questionnaires were excluded from the analysis because of a significant number of incomplete items. The remaining 228 usable responses constituted the data for analysis.

Results of Study 3

The mean importance ratings for the 28 statements are presented in Table 5. The mean importance ratings were analysed using the principal components factor analysis, with varimax rotation. Five factors emerged with eigenvalues of greater than 1.0 and coefficient alphas of greater than .50. These five factors accounted for 57.4% of the total variance. Table 6 presents the factor loadings. Factor 1 was defined as "open competition, honest and thorough communication to know job and work team". Six items had high loadings of between .58 and .73 on this factor which accounted for 20.3% of the total variance. Factor 2 was defined as "use of interviews and choice of selectors". Four items had loadings of between .58 and .78 on the factor which accounted for 11.7% of the total variance. Factor 3 was defined as "voice and information soliciting". Four items had loadings between .54 and .70 on this factor . The factor accounted for 10.2% of the total variance. Factor 4 was defined as "bias avoidance and ethicality" with four items having loadings between .53 and .74 on the factor. Approximately 8.5% of the total variance was accounted for by factor 4. The final fifth factor was defined as "use of job-relevant criteria". Two items had high loadings on this factor (.74 and .64). This factor accounted for 6.7% of the total variance. The coefficient alphas for the five factors were .57, .69, .67, .55, and .54 respectively.

Common Determinants of Fair Selection Procedures

An examination of the factors identified in the three studies revealed several common determinants of perceived fairness. This indicates that job candidates, irrespective of the level of the position (i.e., entry-level or managerial positions), shared rather similar perceptions about the fairness of the selection. These common determinants of perceived fairness appear to be in close agreement with Leventhal et al.'s (1980) principles of procedures justice. The principle of following consistent rules is reflected in Factors 1 and 4 in study 1 and 2 respectively. The principle of having opportunities to select the decision-making agent is represented by Factor 1 in studies 1 and 2, and Factor 2 in study 3. The factors honest communication and information soliciting identified in the three studies represent procedures that ensure the use of correct

Table 5
Mean importance ratings: Study 3

Determinants	Mean (SD) (N = 228)	
1. Use impartial interviewers	6.06	(2.77)
2. Conduct job analysis to clearly identify the criteria required to perform in the job and use only the identified job criteria in selection	7.44	(1.96)
3. Company is honest in discussing its weaknesses and future plans for change	8.05	(1.81)
4. Use past work experience as a criterion	7.18	(1.74)
5. Careful cross check of references and qualifications	7.56	(2.26)
6. Make sure that the present job incumbent is not on selection panel so that applicant can freely express ideas for changes in the way the position should be handled	7.19	(2.58)
7. Use quantified method by assigning check points to each applicant for objective comparisons	5.84	(2.41)
8. Chance to meet all the staff in the work group to check compatibility before deciding to take the job	4.99	(2.77)
9. Use interviews in gathering information	7.08	(2.42)
10. Advertise every position for open competition	5.98	(2.80)
11. Use job-related competence as key criterion	7.28	(1.79)
12. Avoid using nepotism	7.93	(2.48)
13. Use group of interviewers in interviews	4.81	(2.83)
14. Detailed feedback to know selection was carefully carried out	6.19	(2.41)
15. Use academic qualifications as criterion	5.35	(2.08)
16. Chance to let applicant make a case for him/herself in the selection process	8.38	(1.60)
17. Use psychological tests in selection	4.88	(2.63)
18. Avoid personality as criterion in selection	4.02	(2.48)
19. Equal opportunity regardless of sex, age, or race	7.10	(2.92)
20. Use same selection procedure for every applicant	7.91	(2.35)
21. Clear, honest two-way communication in interviews for applicant to get a realistic picture of job	9.26	(1.02)
22. Employer has not made a decision before the interview	9.20	(1.57)
23. Have equal number of male and female interviewers on panel	2.34	(2.44)
24. Use competent interviewers	8.44	(1.89)
25. Avoid using looks as a criterion	6.03	(2.99)
26. Collect recommendations or references in addition to application forms	7.28	(2.41)
27. Chance to meet the boss or supervisor before deciding to take the job	8.57	(1.89)
28. Allow sufficient time for interviews	9.13	(1.00)

SDs in parentheses

information in selections. The factors ethicality and bias avoidance reflect Leventhal et al.'s (1980) procedural principles of using prevailing moral and ethical standards and using safeguards against bias. The only procedural principle in Leventhal et al.'s theory that was not evident in the present results is that of correctability of decision which allows provisions for appeals against the final decision. It appears that this principle is not regarded as a key factor of fairness in personnel selection procedures.

The fairness determinants of selection procedures that are common to all three studies deserve further discussion. The first common determinant concerns honest and thorough communication from the organization about the job. The key components of this determinant appear to be "honest interaction", "provision of realistic job information", and "provision of decision feedback". The honest interaction component reflects Bies and Moag's (1986) concern for interactional justice in a recruiting setting. The importance of interactional justice in situations involving social communications has been well established (Folger, 1988; Lane, 1988b; Lind & Tyler, 1988). Since the selection process could be construed as an interactional process between candidates and recruiters, it is not surprising that job candidates are concerned with the qualities of such interactions. The present findings showed that job applicants would feel that they were fairly treated if the employer was honest in describing the nature of the job, and in providing detailed feedback about the selection. The provision of realistic job information is important for the candidates because realistic information about job attributes could significantly affect their final reactions to job offers and job acceptance (Taylor & Bergmann, 1987), as well as their post entry job satisfaction and survival (e.g., Premack & Wanous, 1985; Wanous, 1989). The importance of feedback provision at work has been well established (e.g., Becker & Klimoski, 1989). In the present studies, candidates further considered getting detailed feedback about the selection process an important criterion of a fair selection procedure.

The second common determinant of a fair selection procedure concerns the selection interview. Candidates considered fair selection procedures as involving the conduct of interviews by a group of competent and impartial interviewers. The importance of the interview in the selection practice (e.g., Eder & Buckley, 1988) as well as the impact of interviewers on applicants have been well documented. For instance, it has been shown that candidates' perceptions of the interviewers had significant impact on their regard for the job and the organization, as well as their decision to accept the job offer (e.g., Harris & Fink, 1987; Taylor & Bergmann, 1987; Phillip & Dipboye, 1989). The use of board or panel interviews has already been recommended by Arvey and Campion (1982) as a way of improving the validity and reliability of the interviews.

The third common determinant of a fair selection practice concerns the process of soliciting information about the candidates. Specifically, the respondents believed that a fair information soliciting process should involve inputs from candidates themselves; and a thorough search of candidates' concise qualifications. The importance of "voice" procedures in legal and organizational decision making is the subject of several recent studies. Voice procedures are perceived as fairer than non-voice or "mute" procedures (e.g., Bies & Shapiro, 1988; Folger & Greenberg, 1985; Greenberg & Folger, 1983; Lind et al., 1990). Candidates in the present studies also considered voice as an important determinant of procedural fairness in selection. In addition, fair selection decisions are more likely to achieve if evaluations of candidates are based on thorough and concise informations about each candidates.

The fourth fairness determinant is about the avoidance of biases in the selection procedures. Respondents believed that a fair selection decision should not be affected by candidates' non-job related characteristics including sex, age, looks or personality; nor should the decision be affected by the personal relationships between the recruiters and the candidates. However, as reviewed in Chapter 3, there has been ample evidence of the significant impact of candidate sex, age or race on selection interview decisions. Furthermore, applicant personality has been shown to be the interviewers" focal point in the interview process (e.g., Rothstein & Jackson, 1984). Several personality dimensions such as social difficulty, locus of control and machiavellianism, (e.g., Keenan, 1982) and extroversion (Fletcher, 1987) have been found to have an effect on interview evaluation outcomes. Paunonen, Jackson, and Aberman (1987) also found that interviewers used job-personality fit as a criterion in their candidate evaluations. Applicant appearance has also been a significant criterion used by interviewers in job assessment (e.g., Kinicki & Lockwood, 1985; Dickey-Bryant, Lautenschlager, Mendoza & Abrahams, 1986).

The answer to the question of whether specific personality dimensions should be included as selection criteria would ultimately depend on the evidence of their job-relatedness and the construct validity of the measures used (Guion, 1987). Traditional personality or temperament variables have been shown to be poor predictors of job proficiency (e.g., Hunter & Hunter, 1984).

43

However, the recently developed "construct-oriented" personality measures have significant validities in predicting job performance (e.g., Hough, 1988; Pulakos, Borman & Hough, 1988). Several other studies have also reported significant validities of various personality measures in predicting job performance (e.g., Love & O'Hara, 1987; Ash, Baehr, Joy & Orban, 1988; Ferris, Bergin & Gilmore, 1986). While Blinkhorn and Johnson (1990) presented evidence on the insignificance of personality testing in the evaluation of job applicants, Barrick and Mount (1991) provided meta-analysis data on significant predictive validities of five personality dimensions (extraversion, emotional stability, agreeableness, conscientiousness, and openness to experience) in predicting job proficiency.

The fifth common determinant of a fair selection procedure concerns the use of job-relevant competence and past work experience as criteria. It has been shown that work experience was consistently used as a criterion in selection decisions (e.g., Singer & Bruhns, 1991). Although studies on criterion validation have shown that candidate academic qualification is another significant job-relevant predictor of managerial performance (e.g., Howard, 1986), the item "use academic qualification as a criterion" was regarded only by entry-level applicants as a key determinant of fairness (Factor 1 of Study 1). This item did not emerge in the key factors identified by the managerial respondents in study 2 or study 3. This appears consistent with Miner's (1976) survey data indicating that managers typically gave academic qualification low weight in selection decisions.

In addition to factor analysis comparisons, a comparison in terms of mean importance ratings of the three samples also deserve attention. Such a comparison (Tables 1,3 and 5) revealed that all samples attached the highest importance to selection procedures such as "clear, honest communication for applicants to get a realistic picture of job" and "employer has not made a decision before the interview". However, unlike applicants for entry-level jobs, managerial candidates also considered "allow sufficient time for interviews" and "chance to meet the boss or supervisor before deciding to take the job" among the most important determinants of a fair selection practice. Despite these minor differences, the overall pattern of results seems to indicate that entry-level and managerial candidates share rather similar perceptions about the fairness of a selection practice.

44

Consequences of Fairness Perceptions About Selection Procedures

The study of the effect of fairness perceptions about selection procedures on candidates' later job attitudes represents a "quasi-longitudinal" approach. Such an approach has been advocated independently in the selection and the procedural justice literatures. In recent selection literature, Herriot (1989) argued that selection research should conceptualize selection process as the first stage of a continuing social interaction process between the organization and the applicant. A similar view was expressed earlier by Wanous (1980) in the context of the effect of realistic job previews on applicant post entry socialization. It was also suggested that selection research should take into account selection effects of a longer time span such as applicants' organizational entry adjustment (Taylor & Bergmann, 1987; Robertson & Smith, 1989). Several studies have taken this approach in examining the effects of candidates' perceptions about recruiters on their post-selection attitudes towards the job and organization (e.g., Harris & Fink, 1987; Phillip & Dipboye, 1989; Taylor & Bergmann, 1987). In selection involving assessment centres, it was found that assessment centre evaluations also significantly affected candidates' subsequent career attitudes and career behaviors (Noe & Steffy, 1987; Fletcher, 1991).

From the procedural justice literature, Lind and Tyler (1988) have explicitly argued that the real proof of the value of the procedural justice perspective lies in its power to generate new testable hypotheses such as possible behavioral consequences of procedural fairness perceptions. It has been shown that perceptions of procedural fairness had a significant impact on job satisfaction (Alexander & Ruderman, 1987; Lissak, Mendes, & Lind, 1983), evaluation of supervisors (Alexander & Ruderman, 1987; Greenberg, 1987c; Kanfer, Sawyer, Earley & Lind, 1987), as well as trust in management (Alexander & Ruderman, 1987). Lind and Tyler (1988) further hypothesized that procedural fairness perceptions would also impact on employees' "attitudes toward the organization as a whole, including such things as organizational commitment, loyalty and work group cohesiveness" (p.179). With reference to impact on organizational commitment, three recent studies examined the impact of fairness perceptions about an organization's layoff procedures on survivors' organizational commitment (Brockner, 1990; Brockner, DeWitt, Grover & Reed, in press; Greenberg, 1990). It was found that fairness perceptions significantly affected survivors' organizational commitment;

45

however, the effect was moderated by survivors' scope of justice regarding the layoff victims.

In the selection literature, studies taking such a quasi-longitudinal approach have focused on the impact of candidates' perceptions about the recruiters or the impact of the actual selection decisions, no study to date has examined the impact of candidates' perceptions about the *fairness* of selection procedures. Study 4 addresses such an issue.

Subjects and Procedures of Study 4

This study was an extension of the postal survey research reported in study 3. The research questionnaire consisted of 34 items. Of these, 28 items involves the same statements as those used in study 3. Subjects were asked to think of a recent and specific occasion when they applied for a managerial position. They were asked to go through the 28 statements and to rate each statement in terms of the extent to which it "accurately represented" the actual selection procedures used by the recruiting organization on that occasion. The ratings were made on the same 11-point scale ranging from "not at all representative of the specific selection occasion" (0) to "extremely representative of the specific selection occasion" (10). They were then asked whether they were offered the position, whether they took the offer, and how long they were in that position for.

The other six items in the questionnaire assessed later job attitudes about this position. Of the six items, two assessed organizational commitment: "How much do you think that you are committed to your present work?" and "How much do you feel like continuing to work for this company/firm for the next few years?" Two items assessed work satisfaction: "How satisfied are you with the kind of work you are doing in this position?" and "How happy are you with the conditions of your work such as pay and supervision?". Two items assessed perceptions of organizational effectiveness: "In your view, how effective is this company /firm?" and "In your view, how efficient is the general functioning or management of this company/firm?".

The questionnaire was posted to the same randomly selected pool of 680 male professional managers as described in study 3. Altogether 118 of the 228 subjects in study 3 also completed this questionnaire. Of the 118 respondents, six were not offered the position they described, and two turned down the offer. Because of the absence of the data on job attitudes, these eight responses were excluded from this study. The following analyses were therefore based on the data of the remaining 110 respondents.

Results of Study 4

For each respondent, five factor scores were calculated. The five factor scores were based on the five fairness determinants emerged from the factor analysis in study 3 (see Table 6). Because the same 28 statements were used in the questionnaire used for study 4, each of the five factor scores was calculated by averaging respondents' ratings of all the corresponding items having significant loadings on that factor. These factor scores can then be used to index respondents' fairness perceptions about the specific managerial selection practice they recently experienced.

To test the impact of fairness perceptions on successful candidates' later job attitude, the five factor scores were used as predictor scores (independent variables) in three multiple regression analyses against the three dependent variables of organizational commitment, work satisfaction and perceived organizational effectiveness. Table 7 presents the intercorrelations among all variables and results of the regression analyses. The regression analysis against the organizational commitment variable yielded an R of .72, adjusted R^2 = .50, $F(5,102)$ = 22.15, $p<.01$. This variable was significantly predicted by Factor 1,"open competition, honest and thorough communication to know job and work team" (B = .54, p <.01), Factor 3, "voice and information soliciting" (B =.31, $p<.01$), and Factor 5, "use of job-relevant criteria" (B = .16, $p<.05$). The regression analysis against the work satisfaction variable showed an R of .76, adjusted R^2 = .56, $F(5,102)$ = 28.42, $p<.01$. This variable was predicted by Factor 1 (B =.52, $p<.01$) and Factor 3 (B =.28, $p<.01$). The regression analysis against the perceived organizational effectiveness criterion yielded an R of .70, adjusted R^2 =.49, $F(5,102)$ = 19.93, $p<.01$. Factor 1 was the only significant predictor of this variable, B=.65, $p<.01$.

Discussion

Table 7 shows that, except Factor 4 (bias avoidance and ethicality), all other factors of procedural fairness identified by managerial candidates, were significantly correlated with these candidates' later organizational commitment, work satisfaction and perceptions of organizational effectiveness. However, results of the regression analyses revealed that only Factor 1, "open competition, honest and

47

Table 6

Factor analysis and item factor loadings in study 3

Factors	F1	F2	F3	F4	F5
Factor 1: "Open Competition, Honest and Thorough Communication to Know Job and Work Team"					
Clear, honest two-way communication in interviews for applicants to get a realistic picture of job	.73				
Advertise every position for open competition	.72				
Detailed feedback to know selection was carefully carried out	.70				
Employer has not made a decision before the interview	.63				
Chance to meet all the staff in the work group to check compatibility before deciding to take the job	.60				
Chance to meet the boss or supervisor before deciding to take the job	.58				
Factor 2: "Use of Interviews and Choice of Selectors"					
Use group of interviewers in interviews		.78			
Use interviews in gathering information		.70			
Use competent interviewers		.64			
Use impartial interviewers		.58			
Factor 3: "Voice" and "Information Soliciting"					
Chance to let applicant make a case for him/herself in the selection process			.70		
Collect recommendations or references in addition to application forms			.69		
Careful cross check of references and qualifications			.58		
Allow sufficient time for interviews			.54		
Factor 4: "Bias Avoidance" and "Ethicality"					
Avoid using looks as a criterion				.74	
Avoid personality as a criterion in selection				.68	
Equal opportunity regardless of sex, age or race				.59	
Avoid using nepotism				.53	
Factor 5: "Use of Job-Relevant Criteria"					
Use job-relevant competence as key criterion					.74
Use past work experience as a criterion					.64
Eigenvalue	5.67	3.26	2.84	2.37	1.87
Percentage of variance	20.3	11.7	10.2	8.5	6.7

Note: Only factor loadings of .50 or larger are shown

Table 7

Intercorrelations among all variables and multiple regression analyses using factor scores as predictors of commitment, satisfaction, and perceived effectiveness: Study 4

Variables	1	2	3	4	5	6	7	8	Multiple Regression					
									Organizational commitment		Work satisfaction		Perceived effectiveness	
									β	t	β	t	β	t
1. Factor 1 score	(.57)	.45**	.56**	.22**	.32**	.71**	.66**	.70**	.54**	6.21**	.52**	3.37**	.65**	7.25**
2. Factor 2 score		(.69)	.23**	.14	.29**	.36**	.32**	.35**	.16*	2.15*	.12	1.74	.08	.85
3. Factor 3 score			(.67)	.17	.23**	.60**	.55**	.45**	.31**	3.42**	.28**	3.37**	.14	.98
4. Factor 4 score				(.55)	.15	.08	.07	.13	-.14	-1.79	-.06	-.85	-.03	-.35
5. Factor 5 score					(.54)	.18*	.34**	.31**	.02	.18	.14	1.73	.06	.69
6. Organizational commitment						(.80)	.83**	.77**						
7. Work satisfaction							(.78)	.76**						
8. Perceived organizational effectiveness								(.84)						

Note: Coefficient alphas for each factor and the inter-item Pearson correlations for the three dependent variables are in parentheses.

* p < .05   ** p < .01

Source: Tables 5 to 7 inclusive originally appeared in *Social Justice Research*, 1992, 5, pp. 49-70.

49

thorough communication to know job and work team", consistently and significantly predicted all three job attitude variables. Factor 3, "voice and information soliciting", was also a significant predictor of the two job variables of commitment and satisfaction. Factor 2, "use of interview and choice of selectors", made a significant but minor contribution to the variable of commitment. Neither Factor 4, "bias-avoidance and ethicality", nor Factor 5, "use of job-relevant criteria", was predictive of any of the three candidate variables.

The consistent and robust effect of Factor 1, could be interpreted in part by the realistic job information theory (Kirnan, Farley & Geisinger, 1989; Wanous, 1989). This theory asserts that candidates given realistic job information tend to develop realistic expectations about the job and hence are more likely to survive on the job. Empirical evidence has shown that realistic job previews could impact on turnover rates and satisfaction with job (e.g., McEvoy & Cascio, 1985; Meglino & DeNisi, 1987; Miceli, 1985; Premack & Wanous, 1985). In the context of selection, the present findings further showed that the more the organization was open and honest in its communication with managerial candidates, the more they would later feel committed to the organization and satisfied with their work; and the more likely they would perceive the organization as being effective.

The fairness factor of voice and information soliciting was also predictive of commitment and satisfaction. The importance of voice lies in its being the key element of process control (Lind et al., 1990; Thibaut & Walker, 1978). Previous research has established positive effects of voice procedures on job satisfaction among federal employees (Alexander & Ruderman, 1987) and Armed Forces (Lissak, Mendes, & Lind, 1983); as well as on performance appraisal in laboratory studies (Greenberg, 1987c; Kanfer, Sawyer, Earley, & Lind, 1987). Study 3 has further extended the voice effects to include work satisfaction and organizational commitment in a managerial selection context.

Neither of Factor 4," bias avoidance and ethicality", nor Factor 5, "use of job-relevant criteria", had a significant effect on candidate job attitudes. A closer examination of these two factors revealed that both were about the "selection criteria". These two factors together specified the sorts of selection criteria that decision makers (i.e., recruiters) "should" (Factor 5) and "should not" (Factor 4) use in their selection decisions. These factors were therefore termed "decision factors". In contrast, the other three procedural factors were primarily about "process criteria" in selection procedures.

Specifically, Factor 1 was mainly concerned with the communication and feedback processes; Factor 2, the information soliciting processes; and Factor 3, the interviewing and interviewer choice processes.

The distinction between decision and process factors parallels to that between "decision control" and "process control" in Thibaut and Walker 's (1978) original theory; decision control was conceptualised as the more decisive means in assuring fair outcomes. Individuals resort to rely on process controls when they recognize that direct control over final decisions was unattainable or impractical. Process controls are hence indirect means in assuring the fairness of final outcomes. In the present context of managerial selection, fair selection decisions are most likely to be made if recruiters would use appropriate selection decision criteria (i.e., decision factors) in their evaluations. Relative to the process factors (Factors 1,2 and 3), controls over recruiters' use of decision criteria (Factors 4 and 5) are therefore more instrumental in achieving fair selection decisions.

Despite the greater instrumentality value of the decision factors in achieving desired final outcomes, the present findings suggest that candidates' perceptions of having controls over decision factors had no effect on their later job attitudes. Job attitudes were only affected by perceptions about process factors. A similar pattern of results has been reported in studies directly comparing the effects of decision factors and process factors (e.g., Lind, Lissak, & Conlon, 1983; Tyler, 1987). These findings are therefore convergent in suggesting that controls over process may serve purposes other than the assurance of fair outcomes. Assurance of fair outcomes may not be as important a concern for candidates as assurance of personal involvement in terms of opportunities to express one's views in the selection procedures. The findings could therefore be seen as supportive of Lind and Tyler's (1988) assertion that issues of process are more important than issues of outcome.

5 Applying outcome justice notions to selection research

The question of whether the outcome of a selection decision is fair or not is most relevant in practices whereby not the best qualified (according to job-relevant qualifications or experiences) candidate gets the job offer. These practices typically involve preferential selection or quota hiring. Preferential selection or quota hiring refers to selection decisions that are based primarily on job-irrelevant factors such as applicant gender, age or ethnicity. Relevant qualifications or merits which are predictive of job performance receive only secondary consideration. Conceptually preferential selection represents a special case of resources allocation whereby employment opportunities are distributed in the manner prescribed by rules of preferential selection. Because the allocation rules of preferential selection are not based on job-relevant merits, they are therefore contradicting the widely held belief that fair selections abide by the principle of meritocracy. In this context, the issue of the justice or fairness of preferential selection is at stake.

Outcome Fairness and Preferential Selection

In the ethics literature, the rights and wrongs of preferential selection have been the subject of intense debate over the last two decades. Proponents of the selection program put forward three major justifications: First, preferential selection obeys the compensatory justice principle and is a form of compensation to the minorities for past discriminations they have suffered (e.g., Minas, 1977; Taylor, 1973). Second, preferential selection is a means to promote social welfare and to achieve distributive justice in future employment opportunities (e.g., Sher, 1975). Third, preferential selection helps broadening the talent pool of organizations by utilizing minority talents (e.g., Shaw, 1988). Opponents have argued against the program on four grounds: First, compensation for past ills should not be required of all members of majority groups, nor should reparation go to all members of minority groups (e.g., Goldman, 1975). Second, preferential selection itself violates the principle of equality by discriminating against white males (e.g., Newton, 1973). Third, selection should be based on job-relevant merits or qualifications rather than on irrelevant factors (e.g., Garrett & Klonoski, 1986). Fourth, preferential selection implies that minorities are inferior hence are in need of help (e.g., Goldman, 1976), and that real achievements of minorities may be denigrated (e.g., Shaw, 1988).

The focus of the psychological literature of preferential selection differs between gender-based and ethnicity-based selections. The literature on gender-based selection tends to focus on the program's individual and societal consequences. At the individual level, it was found that sex-based preferential treatment in selection of leaders had a negative impact on subordinates' judgements of leader performance (Jacobson & Koch, 1977). Women's jobs were devalued when others thought that their selections were based on preferential treatment (Heilman & Herlihy, 1984). Sex-based selection also had a negative effect on women's organizational commitment, job satisfaction and role stress (Chacko, 1982), as well as on women's self-perceptions and self-evaluations of their own task performance (Heilman, Simon & Repper, 1987). Sex-based selection further left female selectees feeling stigmatized, such "procedural stigma" resulted in the woman's experience of evaluation apprehension (Nacoste, & Lehman, 1987).

More recent studies however have shown that sex-based selection does not uniformly induce negative self-evaluations among women. Such self-devaluating consequences were only found among women when they had doubts in their own performance effectiveness (Heilman, Lucas & Kaplow,1990), when they perceived such selections as unfair in the first place (Nacoste, 1989), and when information about such sex-based selection was left ambiguous (Heilman,Rivero & Brett,1991).

At the societal level, recent longitudinal studies showed that among African Americans, these programs created not only a great disparity between the two sexes in social and economic advancement (Bell, 1989), but also feelings of uncertainty and psychological stress from various fronts in the society, for those women who had benefited from the program (Garcia, 1989).

The literature on ethnicity-based preferential selection has focused on the psychometric, utility and differential ability issues examined previously in Chapter 3. The conclusion appears to be that the goals of optimising organizational productivity and quota hiring are in conflict (e.g., Schmitt, 1989). In addition, there has been evidence that most white Americans are not in favour of such preferential treatment (Kluegel & Smith, 1983; Lipset & Schneider, 1978). In a recent national survey, Kinder and Sanders (1990) found that white Americans in general opposed to ethnicity-based preferential treatment in selection, regardless of whether the question was framed in terms of reverse discrimination or unfair advantage.

These findings are therefore convergent in suggesting that preferential selection, based on either candidate gender or ethnicity, may have adverse psychological, organizational and societal consequences. However, Crosby and Clayton (1990) recently argued that while affirmative action programs can have negative effects on interpersonal and intrapersonal expectancies; such negative effects are by no means inevitable. Furthermore, Effectively implemented affirmative action programs can be advantageous for the intended target groups and can help promote true equality of opportunity in society.

Although consideration of justice is fundamental to preferential selection, only limited research has provided direct empirical data on individuals' justice or fairness perceptions of the outcomes of preferential selection. Nacoste (1987) showed that when female subjects played the role of the female appointee, they perceived selections based solely on gender as less fair than selections placing equal weight on their qualifications and gender. The fairness ratings reported in Heilman et.al. (1991) revealed that although men perceived sex-based selection as unfair, women perceived such selections as significantly less unfair. However, no such data are yet available on ethnicity-based selections. Studies 5 and 6 report data on individuals' outcome fairness perceptions about both gender-based and ethnicity-based selections. Study 5 employs a within-subjects design and study 6, a between-subjects design.

A selection questionnaire was designed for this study. Respondents were required to evaluate the fairness of 22 cases of selection outcomes. The following instructions were given:

"This survey is about individuals' perceptions of fairness in selection decisions for a vocational training course. We would like you to put yourself in the shoes of the training director who is solely responsible for selecting candidates for the course. Candidates are required to sit for a general training test. Selection decisions are primarily based on candidates' scores on the test. The training director is concerned about the fact that, not many females (or " ethnic-minority members" for the ethnicity-based selection case) have been selected for this training course. His overall concern is for a fair approach to selection. In each of the following items, you will be given the general training test scores of two candidates as well as the selection decisions of the training director. You are required to evaluate on a seven-point scale the fairness of each decision. The general training test scores are out of 100. The mean score is 61. In each item, candidate B is a female (or "an ethnic-minority member" for the ethnicity-based selection case), and candidate A is a male (or "of European origin").

Respondents were then required to rate the fairness of each decision on a 7-point rating scale with "1" labelled as "extremely unfair" and "7" as "extremely fair". For example, one item reads:

"Candidate A: 64

Candidate B: 68

Candidate A is a male (or "of European origin" for the ethnicity-based selection case), and candidate B is a female (or "a member of an ethnic-minority group").

The training director selected candidate A".

Four types of selection outcomes constituted 20 items in the questionnaire: candidate A had a higher trainability score who also was selected ("A > B / Select A"); Candidate A had a higher trainability score but candidate B was selected ("A > B / select B"); candidate B had a higher trainability score who was also selected ("A < B / select B"); and candidate B had a higher score but candidate A was selected ("A < B / select A"). The other two items in the questionnaire represented these two cases: ("A = B / select A") and ("A = B / select B"). Among these four types of outcomes, both ("A > B / select A") and ("A < B / select B") represented selections based on "performance-relevant merits" alone. Given that candidate B was a minority member, the outcome ("A < B /

select A") represented conventional discrimination against minority candidates; whereas the outcome ("A > B / select B") represented preferential selection or reverse discrimination in selection.

There were two independent variables in the study.

1. The categories to which the minority candidate belonged. Half of the respondents were told that candidate B was a female and candidate A was a male (the "female-minority" category); the other half of the respondents were told that candidate B was a member of a minority ethnic group and candidate A belonged to the ethnic majority group (the "ethnic-minority" category).

2. The size of the discrepancy between the two candidates' trainability scores. For each of the four types of outcomes, five discrepancy scores (4, 8, 12, 16 and 20) were used to represent the differences in trainability scores. It was hypothesized that the level of perceived fairness (or unfairness) of selection outcomes would be significantly affected by the magnitude of discrepancy in merits between the chosen minority and the unsuccessful majority candidate.

Subjects and Procedures of Study 5

Altogether 222 (83 males and 139 females) undergraduate psychology students took part in this study. All subjects were European New Zealanders (eleven responses from ethnic minority subjects were excluded from the analysis). The mean age was 20 years and 9 months.

The selection questionnaire was given out and completed in subjects' tutorial classes. The size of these classes ranged between 20 and 32. A female master's thesis student conducted the survey and debriefed the subjects. The task took up to 20 minutes to complete.

Results of Study 5

In data analyses, four mean fairness ratings for the four types of selection outcomes (i.e., "A > B / select A"; "A > B / select B"; "A < B / select A"; and "A < B / select B") were calculated for each subject. The sample means are presented in Table 8.

To test whether males perceived gender-based selection outcomes as unfair, male respondents' mean fairness rating for the "female-minority" category and the outcome ("A>B /select B"), (mean = 2.20) was compared to a null mean of 4 (the neutral point on the 7-point scale), $t(43)=8.39$, $p<.01$. This indicates that males did

Table 8
Mean fairness ratings for the four types of selection decisions: Study 5

"Minority category"	"Sex of subjects"	"Candidate score"	"Decision"	
			Select A	Select B
"Female-minority"	M (N = 44)	A > B	5.67 (1.10)	2.20 (1.21)
		A < B	2.08 (.99)	5.87 (1.21)
	F (N = 70)	A > B	5.83 (1.21)	2.27 (1.19)
		A < B	2.11 (1.11)	6.03 (1.18)
"Ethnic-minority"	M (N = 39)	A > B	5.65 (1.19)	2.34 (1.17)
		A < B	2.20 (1.07)	5.84 (1.07)
	F (N = 69)	A > B	5.73 (1.20)	2.42 (1.22)
		A < B	2.07 (1.11)	5.81 (1.13)

SDs in parentheses

Source: Originally published in *Current Psychology: Research and Reviews*, 1992, 11, pp 128-144. Published by Transaction Publishers. The same source applies to Figure 1.

perceive sex-based selection as unfair. To test whether whites perceived ethnicity-based selection as unfair, the mean fairness rating by all respondents (Europeans) for the "ethnic-minority" category and the outcome ("A>B/select B"), (mean = 2.39), was also compared to the neutral point of 4, $t(107) = 6.82$, $p<.01$. This finding indicates that whites also perceived ethnicity-based selections as unfair.

To check fairness perceptions by the entire sample for all four types of decisions, each of the 16 cell means in Table 8 was compared with the null mean of 4, all 16 comparisons yielded significant results ($p<.05$). This indicates that all merit-based decisions were perceived as fair and that all selection decisions based on candidate sex or ethnicity were perceived as unfair. Further, the two merit-based decisions, ("A > B / select A") and ("A < B / select B"),were perceived as equally fair for both minority categories. The mean fairness ratings (irrespective of sex of subjects) were 5.78 ("A > B / select A") and 5.96 ("A < B / select B"), $t(113) = 1.09$ for the "female-minority" category; and 5.70 ("A > B / select A") and 5.82 ("A < B / select B"), $t(107) = .92$ for the "ethnic-minority" category. In addition, results of the comparison between preferential selection ("A > B / select B") and discrimination against minority group ("A < B / select A") showed that these two types of discrimination were perceived as equally unfair for both minority categories. For "female-minority" category, the means were 2.24 and 2.10, $t(107) = .89$ for the two outcomes respectively. For "ethnic-minority" category, the respective means were 2.39 and 2.12, $t(107) = 1.60$.

To test whether "minority-category" had an effect on fairness perception, A 2 (minority category: "female-minority" vs. "ethnic-minority") x 2 (candidate score: "A > B" vs "A < B") x 2 (decision: "select A" vs "select B") analysis of variance (ANOVA) with repeated measures on the last two factors was performed on the fairness ratings. The only significant effect was the "candidate score" x "decision" interaction, $F(1, 220) = 18.97$, $p < .01$. The absence of a significant main effect for "minority category" indicates that fairness perceptions of selection decisions were independent of the type of discriminations involved (i.e., sex or ethnic-minority categories).

To test whether sex of subjects has an effect on fairness perception, a similar 2 (sex of subjects) x 2 (candidate score) x 2 (decision) ANOVA was performed for the two minority categories separately. A similar pattern of results emerged, the only significant effect from each ANOVA was the "candidate score" x

58

"decision" interaction: $F(1, 112) = 19.97$, $p < .01$ for the "female-minority" category; and $F(1, 106) = 17.13$, $p < .01$ for the "ethnic minority" category. Neither the main "sex of subjects" effect nor any interaction involving this variable was found significant. This indicates that male and female subjects had similar fairness perception of selection outcomes.

To test the hypothesis that perceived outcome fairness would be significantly affected by the magnitude of the score discrepancy between the two candidates, the mean fairness ratings for the 11 score discrepancies (A-B = +20, +16, +12, +8, +4, 0, -4, -8, -12, -16, and -20) were calculated separately for the two decisions of "select A" and "select B." This was because the result of hypothesis 1 showed that a significant interaction existed between "candidate score" and "decision" in fairness ratings. Figure 1 presents the relationship between fairness ratings and score discrepancies. A single factor (i.e., score discrepancies) ANOVA with repeated measures was performed on the fairness ratings for the two decisions ("select A" vs "select B") and the two minority categories separately. For "female-minority" category, $F(1, 113) = 13.17$, $p < .01$ ("select A") and $F(1, 113) = 17.01$, $p < .01$ ("select B"). For "ethnic-minority" category, $F(1, 107) = 19.97$, $p < .01$ ("select A") and $F(1, 107) = 19.92$, $p < .01$ ("select B"). These results support the hypothesis that outcome fairness perceptions about both gender-based and ethnicity-based selections were significantly affected by the size of the candidates' score discrepancies.

Design of Study 6

In study 5, outcome fairness perceptions were examined in a within-subjects context whereby each respondent made fairness judgements of 22 cases of selection decisions including both merit-based and preferential selections. The finding that preferential selection outcomes were perceived as unfair, might be in part due to subjects' making direct comparisons between these outcomes and those which were merit-based. Social psychological research has shown that because of the possibility of such comparisons in within-subjects studies, relevant effect sizes are typically larger than those in between-subjects designs (e.g., Olian, Schwab & Haberfeld, 1988). In this study, a between-subjects design was used to cross check whether, in the absence of a merit-based selection context, outcomes of preferential selection would still be perceived as unfair.

A selection decision questionnaire was designed for this study.

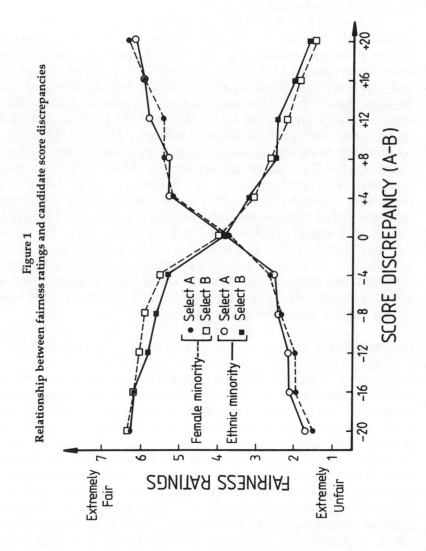

Figure 1

Relationship between fairness ratings and candidate score discrepancies

The questionnaire consisted of a hypothetical case describing the recruiting process and the final selection decision for a position in a consultancy firm, followed by 11 items assessing respondents' evaluation of the selection decision, and either 1 or 3 items for manipulation checks. Here is the hypothetical selection case:

"This case concerns the recruiting practice of a large computer consultancy firm. The firm advertised a position for a computer programmer. All applicants were required to sit for the Computer Programmer Aptitude Test (CPAT) which was specially designed by personnel selection experts for the firm. Previous research has shown that the test is a valid predictor of later job performance. Each candidate's CPAT score was then combined with his/her academic records as well as relevant work experience to form an "overall-merit" score. The top 10 scorers on the overall-merit measure were then interviewed by the personnel department. Here are the names of the 10 final candidates, together with their overall-merit scores (out of 100):

John H (95), Sarah S (90), Bruce M (86), Jerry T (81), Alan B (75), Don T (72), Rob A (67), Paul P (61), Steve N (56), Susan D (50).

All candidates were between 21 and 23 years of age. All had a B.Sc. degree and a similar academic record. All candidates had some previous working experience, but none of them had worked as a computer programmer or in a related job.

The position was offered to Sarah S"

Respondents were then required to go through 11 items evaluating the case. Five dependent variables were assessed by the 11 items: (1) "Outcome fairness" was assessed by three items including " In your view, how would most people judge the fairness of the decision?" (2) "Appointee fairness" was assessed by two items including "In your view, how would Sarah S. judge the fairness of the decision makers?" (3) "Performance effectiveness" of the successful candidate was measured by two items such as "In your view, how likely is Sarah S. going to be an effective member of staff in this consultancy firm?" (4) "Future expectation" assessed future employment expectations of the rejected candidate(s) who scored higher than Sarah S. This variable was measured by two items including "For the rejected candidate(s) who scored higher than Sarah S., how high would his (their) expectations be for getting a similar job offer in the future?" and (5) "Repetition of appointment" was measured by two items assessing the likelihood of Sarah S.' being appointed again. One item was: "In your view, how likely would Sarah S. have been appointed if the decision had been made by a different group of people?".

Among these five variables, the key variable concerns outcome fairness. The other variables were included in the hope that the responses would shed light on a greater range of possible effects of preferential selection. Subjects' responses were made on an 11-point rating scale ranging from "extremely unfair" ("ineffective, inconfident, unlikely") ("0"), to "extremely fair" (effective, confident or likely) ("10").

The independent variable of merit discrepancy was manipulated in the hypothetical selection case by placing the successful candidate Sarah S at the 2nd (CPAT score = 90), 4th (81), 7th (67) or the 10th (50) place in the list. For the condition "10", the name Susan D was excluded from the list and the name Simon D was added and placed at the 9th place in the list. The aim was to keep Sarah S as the highest scoring female candidate.

The same questionnaire was used for fairness judgements about ethnicity-based selection. In doing so, the names of Sarah S. and Susan D. were replaced by Fu-Tuk S. and Chie-Min R. throughout the hypothetical selection case and the 11 items used to evaluate the selection outcome.

Subjects and Procedures of Study 6

Two independent subject samples were used for judgements of gender-based and ethnicity-based selection outcomes separately. The subject sample evaluating gender-based selection consisted of 480 respondents (240 males and 240 females). All respondents were either undergraduates in information technology, mathematics, commerce and management at the University of Western Australia, or undergraduates in information systems at WACAE (Edith Cowen University), or computing sciences at Curtin University in Western Australia. The age range was between 17 and 38 with a mean of 19.3 years.

The subject sample evaluating ethnicity-based selection outcomes consisted of 240 (186 male and 54 female) Asian overseas students and 216 (155 male and 61 female) European students. The Asian students were from Hong Kong, Singapore and Malaysia. All students were completing various degrees or postgraduate studies at Curtin University, Murdoch University and the University of Western Australia in Perth, Australia. The age range was between 17 and 42.

Results of Study 6

For each respondent, five scores were calculated for the five dependent measures : outcome fairness, appointee fairness, performance effectiveness, future expectation and repetition of appointment. Each score represented the mean rating of all (or both) items assessing the particular variable. Table 9 presents the the mean ratings.

(A) Results of the Key Variable: Outcome Fairness

To check whether gender-based preferential selection was perceived as fair by male respondents, each of the four mean ratings of outcome fairness (i.e., 4.45, 3.88, 3.01 and 2.37 for the merit discrepancy conditions "2", "4", "7", and "10" respectively) was compared with a null mean of 5 (the neutral point on the 11-point rating scale, representing neither fair nor unfair). A similar analysis was carried out on the mean ratings for the female sample. The means were 4.38, 4.07, 3.52 and 2.98 for the four merit discrepancy conditions. All comparisons were significant at $p<.05$, indicating that regardless of the size of merit discrepancy, all cases of gender-based preferential selection were perceived as unfair by both men and women.

For ethnicity-based selection, to check whether Asians would perceive the selection as unfair, the same analysis was applied to the mean ratings (5.41, 4.58, 4.56, and 3.97 for the four merit discrepancy conditions). The results indicated that Asian respondents considered the decision under the condition "2" as fair, $t(59) =+ 2.31$, $p<.05$; the decision under the condition "4" as neither fair nor unfair, $t(59) =1.98$; and the decisions ("7" and "10") as unfair, $t(59) = -2.28$, $p<.05$; and -3.16, $p<.01$. For the European sample, all four comparisons were significant at $p<.05$. These results indicate that while European respondents considered all cases of ethnicity-based selections as unfair, Asian respondents shared a similar perceptions only when the size of merit discrepancy was large.

In terms of the effect of merit discrepancy on outcome fairness judgements, results for all four respondent groups consistently showed that perceptions of outcome fairness of preferential selection were a function of the size of merit discrepancy; the greater the merit discrepancy, the more unfair the selection outcomes were perceived. For gender-based selection, the F-statistics for the merit discrepancy effect were $F(3,228) = 17.04$, $p<.01$

63

Table 9
Mean ratings: Study 6

Type of selection	Subject sample	Merit discrepancy	Outcome fairness	Appointee fairness	Performance effectiveness	Future expectation	Repetition of appointment
Gender-based	Males	2	4.45	7.45	7.23	5.98	5.78
		4	3.88	7.43	6.98	5.42	5.17
		7	3.01	6.95	5.58	3.73	3.48
		10	2.37	6.10	3.47	3.57	2.77
	Females	2	4.49	7.78	7.97	6.07	6.07
		4	4.07	7.20	7.22	5.87	5.70
		7	3.52	6.92	5.90	4.57	3.57
		10	2.89	6.33	4.98	4.30	3.20
Ethnicity-based	Europeans	2	4.43	7.28	7.07	5.43	5.11
		4	4.79	6.98	6.68	5.36	5.18
		7	3.42	6.77	5.16	3.92	2.74
		10	3.09	6.69	4.24	3.41	2.70
	Asians	2	5.41	7.43	7.36	6.28	6.72
		4	4.85	6.81	6.40	5.94	6.04
		7	4.22	6.45	5.69	4.69	4.48
		10	3.97	6.56	5.00	4.96	3.81

64

(male respondents) and $F(3,228) = 9.74, p < .01$ (female respondents). For ethnicity-based selection, the F-statistics were $F(3,199) = 11.19$, $p < .01$ (European respondents) and $F(3,224) = 7.57$, $p < .01$ (Asian respondents).

(B) Results of Other Dependent Variables

In addition to judgements of outcome fairness, the specific findings regarding the other four dependent variables also deserve discussion. For the variable appointee fairness, results consistently showed that both subject samples held a similar belief that the minority appointee would perceive the decision as fair: For gender-based selection, the means were 6.98 and 7.06 for males and females respectively. For ethnicity-based selection, the means were 6.81 and 6.93 for Asians and Europeans respectively (all means were significantly higher than the neutral point of 5 on the rating scales). These results, together with the finding that these respondents also perceived preferential selection as unfair, seem to suggest that people typically hold the belief that the very beneficiaries of an inequitable allocation are not capable of making an objective assessment of the fairness of the allocation. This thus points to the relative nature of fairness perceptions and the importance of the principle of "veil of ignorance" (Rawls, 1971) and the rule of "impartiality" (Soltan, 1987) in justice judgement.

For the variable performance effectiveness, both groups thought that the appointee would be effective on the job, although Asians' ratings were more favorable than those of Europeans (the means were 6.11 and 5.79 respectively); and females' ratings were also higher than males' (7.06 vs. 5.82). Furthermore, merit discrepancy exerted significant influence on all groups' ratings on this variable, indicating that as the discrepancy in merit increased, all samples judged the minority appointee's potential job performance as less effective.

It has been argued that one of the adverse consequences of feelings of injustice experienced by those disadvantaged by an unfair allocation is lowered expectancies for achieving better outcomes in the future (Crosby, 1976, 1984; Crosby & Clayton, 1990). Results showed that males reported a significantly lower level of future expectations than did females (means were 4.68 vs. 5.20). This could be because men more readily empathized with the rejected majority candidate through gender identity and consequently felt that their own future job prospects could be similarly affected. The same argument could be applied to account for a similar finding for ethnicity-based selection in that Europeans also had a lower level of expectations than did Asians (4.53 vs. 5.46). Cast in this context, the findings could then be seen as being consistent with the suggestion that those disadvantaged by an unfair allocation may lower their expectations for achieving better outcomes in the future.

In terms of the likelihood for the appointment to be repeated, the results showed that, compared with their respective counterparts, female and Asian respondents believed that the appointment was significantly more likely to be repeated. Consistently for both samples, merit discrepancy had a significant effect on ratings of this variable, indicating that as the discrepancy in merit increased, respondents judged it less likely for the appointee to get the job offer again. The findings therefore suggest that although respondents believed that preferential selection decisions are likely to be made frequently, the relative qualifications of the prospective minority appointee should be a key consideration in setting the limits for the preferential treatment.

Merit Discrepancy and Outcome Fairness Perceptions About Preferential Selection

Using a within-subjects design, study 5 showed that outcomes of preferential selections were consistently regarded as unfair, irrespective of whether the preferential treatment was gender-based or ethnicity-based. Moreover, the level of perceived injustice was directly related to the size of discrepancy in merits between the minority appointee and the rejected but more merited majority candidate. As the minority appointee becomes increasingly less qualified than the rejected majority candidate, the more unfair the selection decision was judged.

Results of study 6 replicated these findings with a between-subjects design. The observed merit discrepancy effect is easily explicable by virtue of the fact that as the discrepancy approaches zero, the selection outcome more closely resembles merit selection, which is generally considered as a fair selection practice (e.g., Heilman, et al., 1991).

For gender-based selection, results of both studies indicate that women, the potential beneficiaries of the selection, also shared similar perceptions of injustice as men, the group potentially disadvantaged by it. For ethnicity-based selection, with the exceptions under the conditions of low merit discrepancies (i.e., "2" and "4"), the minority respondents (the potential beneficiaries) also

66

perceived such selection as similarly unfair as European respondents (the potential victims).

In the light of these findings, a number of questions may follow logically: (1) Why do respondents of the disadvantaged majority groups perceive preferential selection as unfair? (2) Why do women and ethnic minorities, the potential beneficiaries, also perceive preferential selection as unjust? and (3) What possible consequences might such perceptions of injustice have on behavior? The answers to these questions may require an appeal to theories of outcome justice.

Applying Relative Deprivation Theory to Preferential Selection

The outcome justice theory that appears most relevant in explaining issues of outcome justice in preferential selection is the theory of relative deprivation (Davies, 1959; Gurr, 1970; Pettigrew, 1967). The theory was originally advanced for social political and economical problems. The theory is concerned with first, an individual's (or individuals') feelings of deprivation resulting from comparing his/her (or their) rewards with those of a comparative referent person (or group); and second, the behavioral effects of such feelings of deprivation. The theory makes the distinction between egoistic deprivation and fraternal or group deprivation (Runciman, 1966; Rhodebeck, 1981). The concept of fraternal or group deprivation is relevant to preferential selection and refers to the discontent stemming from the status of the entire group to which an individual belongs as compared to a referent group.

Empirical evidence of fraternal or group deprivation has been reported on racial inequities in economic status (Sears & McConahay, 1970; Vanneman & Pettigrew, 1972), and gender-based inequities in pay (Crosby, 1984; Martin, 1981; Martin, Price, Bies & Powers, 1979; Moore, 1990), in employment conditions (Crosby, 1982) and in career opportunities (Tougas & Veilleux, 1988; 1989).

In the context of preferential selection, the fraternal or group deprivation concept appears directly relevant to issues of outcome justice. The relative deprivation theory has recently been applied to affirmative action programs aiming at promoting women's career opportunities in areas of salary, selection and promotion (Tougas & Veilleux, 1988, 1989; Veilleux & Tougas, 1989). To apply relative deprivation theory to preferential selection, one fundamental proposition would have to be established empirically, that is, preferential selection does result in feelings of fraternal or group deprivation among those potentially disadvantaged by it. Study 7 was set up to ascertain such a proposition with reference to gender-based preferential selection.

The application of the relative deprivation notion to gender-based selection could also help explain the injustice felt by women. The relative deprivation theory carries the presumption that emotional reactions (i.e., feelings of deprivation or discontent) may follow the cognizance or perceptions of injustice. If it can be established that sex-based preferential selection also induces feelings of deprivation or discontent among women, the theory could then account for women's felt injustice in terms of the notion "relative deprivation on behalf of others" (Runciman, 1966).

The theory could also allow possible behavioral consequences of perceived injustice to be examined within its theoretical framework. The complex model of relative deprivation theory has four components: the distribution pattern, the comparison process, feelings of deprivation and behavioral consequences (Martin, 1981). Upon establishing that gender-based selection causes feelings of deprivation among its potential victims, further research could then examine their behavioral reactions to such feelings of deprivation.

Design of Study 7

In order to establish that gender-based selection causes feelings of deprivation and discount among those potentially disadvantaged by it and among the potential beneficiaries, the same hypothetical selection case used for gender-based selection in study 6 was used for this study. In the evaluation questionnaire, additional items were used to include four measures of the deprivation construct: "deprivation", "discontent", "wanting" and "deserving"(Crosby, 1984; Sweeney, McFarlin & Inderrieden, 1990). Altogether there were 18 items in the questionnaire. Of these, 11 items assessed outcome fairness and the deprivation construct: (1) "outcome fairness" was measured by the same three items used in study 6, (2) "deprivation" was measured by two items including "How much do you think that the highest scoring candidate, John H., might feel that he is deprived of a better outcome?" (3) "discontent" was measured by two items including "In your view, how dissatisfied is John H. with the outcome?" (4) "deserving" was assessed by two items including "How much do you think that the rejected candidate, John H., deserve to get the job?", and (5)"wanting" was measured by two items including "If you were John H., how much would you want the job?"

The remaining items assessed three variables: "appointee performance", "future expectations" and "repetition of appointment". Subjects' responses were made on the same 11-point rating scale with high ratings indicating more fair, more deserving, more wanting, more deprived, more discontent, higher performance, higher expectations and more likely for a repetition of appointment.

Subjects and Procedures of Study 7

A managerial sample was used in this study. Altogether 281 (185 male and 96 female) management professionals participated in the study. At the time of testing, they were completing an MBA degree at one of the universities in Western Australia: UWA, Curtin, Murdoch, Edith Cowen University . Their then current professional positions included human resources manager,training and development educator, management consultant, work site health manager, CEO, sales representative manager, market research officer, computer consultant, and health information manager. Their age range was between 24 to 54 years.

All subjects completed the questionnaire during their class time. A male research assistant carried out all the testing and the debriefing. Subjects were told that the survey was concerned with people's perceptions about the fairness of an organization's job recruitment decisions. On average it took 15 minutes to complete the questionnaire. Subjects were randomly assigned to one of the merit discrepancy conditions.

Results of Study 7

Because of the small sample size, data for the merit discrepancy conditions of "2" and"4" were combined to form one condition representing a "low" level of merit discrepancy, data for the conditions of "7" and "10" were combined to form a second condition representing a "high" level of merit discrepancy.

For each respondent, eight scores were calculated for the eight dependent variables. Each score represented the mean rating of all (or both) items assessing the particular variable. Table 10 presents the mean ratings. To check whether gender-based selection causes feelings of deprivation among men and women, each of the mean ratings of each of the four measures of the deprivation construct was compared with a null mean of 5 for the male and female

Table 10
Mean ratings: Study 7

Subject sample	Merit discrepancy	Outcome fairness	Deserving	Wanting	Deprivation	Discontent	Appointee fairness	Future expectation	Repetition of appointment
					Dependent variables				
Males	Low	3.53	7.15	7.15	7.94	7.81	7.50	6.02	4.97
	High	2.32	7.23	6.70	7.89	7.81	5.38	5.93	3.15
Females	Low	3.49	7.29	7.51	8.22	8.37	7.29	6.37	4.91
	High	2.46	7.32	7.40	8.05	8.12	5.91	6.24	3.27

70

samples separately. All comparisons yields significant results at $\underline{p} <$ .01, indicating that both male and female professionals felt that the rejected male candidate (1) deserved the position, (2) was eager to get the job, (3) felt deprived and (4) felt dissatisfied with the outcome.

To check whether male and female professional also perceived gender-based selection as unfair, each of the mean outcome fairness ratings was compared with the same neutral point of 5. Results of all comparisons were significant at $\underline{p} < .01$, indicating that both male and female professionals considered all cases of gender-based selections as unfair.

To further examine the relationship among fairness and deprivation measures, a multiple regression analysis was carried out with "deprivation" as the dependent variable and the other four measures (fairness, deserving, wanting and discontent) as predictor variables. The results are presented in Table 11. The results indicate that male and female professionals may attach different meanings to the construct deprivation.

An examination of the managers' means in Table 10 further revealed that while managers' outcome fairness perceptions were affected by the level of merit discrepancy, their feelings of deprivation were not so affected. This was interpreted as meaning that unlike fairness perceptions, emotional reactions to sex-based selection may be independent of the size of discrepancy in merits, any practice of preferential treatment in selection would cause feelings of deprivation and discontent.

Results on the other three dependent variables were consistent with those of study 6 using male and female student samples: (1) both male and female professionals believed that the female appointee would perceive the preferential selection outcome as fair, (2) male professionals believed that the rejected but more qualified male candidate would have much lower expectations for future employment prospects, and (3) both male and female professionals believed that the appointment was less likely to be repeated when merit discrepancy was high.

Relative Deprivation and Gender-Based Preferential Selection

For all the measures of the deprivation construct, the results showed, as predicted, that male and female professionals shared similar feelings of deprivation about gender-based selection. Both groups of professionals felt that the rejected candidate was deprived of a better outcome, that the candidate wanted and deserved a better

Table 11
Multiple regression analysis with "deprivation" as dependent variable: Study 7

Predictors	Males		Females	
	β	t	β	t
Fairness	-.16**	-3.19**	-.06	-.75
Deservingness	.19**	3.79**	.09	1.12
Wanting	-.02	-.43	.15	1.72
Discontent	.63**	11.90**	.58**	6.91**
Multiple R	.78		.69	
Adjusted R^2	.59		.46	
F	67.07**		20.50**	
(df)	(4,180)		(4,91)	

* $p < .05$ ** $p < .01$

72

outcome, and the candidate was dissatisfied with the outcome.

In order to make gender comparisons, this study had to use a "scenario" rather than a "self-reporting" approach. Because of this, the observed emotions represent only empathy the professionals experienced towards a "third" person (i.e., the hypothetical candidate). However, because gender represents a dichotomous attribute and hence is an "inalienable inherent trait " (Donaldson & Werhane, 1983), male professionals were likely to identify with the rejected male candidate. Their responses to the selection case might therefore represent a "projection" of their own personal feelings as if they themselves were the candidate in question. Social identity theory contends that in situations of intergroup conflict, an individual's group membership or social identity becomes a salient concern for the person (e.g., Tajfel, 1982; Tajfel & Turner, 1979). In terms of gender-based preferential selection whereby interests of the two gender groups are in direct conflict, it is likely that respondents readily identify with the candidates in the hypothetical selection case through gender-group membership status. This assumption is supported by Singer's (1991) study concerning fairness perceptions of ethnicity-based preferential selection. The results showed that a similar level of injustice was perceived by male respondents taking an objective bystander's perspective and those taking a subjective participant's position. Given this, the present results would suggest that gender-based selections caused feelings of deprivation and discontent among the potentially disadvantaged, male professionals. In a recent study using a self-reporting approach (Veilleux & Tougas, 1989), it was found that male managers reported feelings of deprivation due to affirmative action programs favoring women. The present finding therefore could be seen as consistent with that of Veilleux and Tougas (1989).

Data on the female sample showed that female professionals experienced empathy of deprivation or "deprivation on behalf of others" (Runciman, 1966, 1968). There is further evidence (Table 6 and 7) suggesting that female professionals felt more strongly than male professionals about the rejected male candidate's eagerness to get the job (i.e., "wanting") and dissatisfaction with the outcome (i.e., "discontent").

Results of the regression analysis concerning the link between perceptions of injustice and feeling of deprivation deserve further discussion. The construct of deprivation is composed of a cognitive component (i.e., perception of injustice) and an emotive component (i.e., deprivation, discontent or dissatisfaction) (Runciman, 1966, 1968; Veilleux & Tougas, 1989). The assumption about the association between perceptions of inequity or injustice and an emotional state of tension and disequilibrium was originally made by equity theorists (e.g., Adams, 1965). Data from this study further indicate that the link between fairness and deprivation my be moderated by gender (Table 11). Male professionals' ratings of deprivation were significantly predicted by their ratings of fairness, deserving and discontent. Female professionals' ratings of deprivation, however, could be predicted only from their ratings of discontent. This suggests that male and female professionals may have placed different weight on the factor fairness in their evaluation of whether the rejected candidate was deprived of a better outcome: fairness considerations appear to be a key factor in determining the level of felt deprivation in men's, but not women's reactions to sex-based selection.

This indicates that cognizance or perceptions of injustice may not necessarily precede feelings of deprivation. These findings thus point to the complexity of the underlying processes of "felt deprivation". Further research should ascertain whether it is gender per se, or the status of the individual (victim vs. beneficiary) that determines the fairness-deprivation relationship. Such findings may have significant implications for relative deprivation research in terms of the method used in the measurement of relative deprivation (Tougas, Veilleux, Cere & Boudreault,1989; Veilleux & Tougas, 1989).

Moreover, Crosby (1984) proposed deserving and wanting as the two preconditions for feelings of deprivation. This however only received partial support from the present data based on the regression analysis.

Consequences of Perceptions of Injustice and Feelings of Deprivation on Behavior

Having established that gender-based selection causes feelings of deprivation and discontent among men, the group disadvantaged by it, relative deprivation theory could then be applied to examine relevant behavioral consequences. The theory postulates that feelings of deprivation may lead to reactions that are either individual-oriented or system-oriented (e.g., Crosby, 1976; Martin, 1981). Although it has been suggested that destructive system-oriented reactions to gender-based preferential selection, such as social unrest, is unlikely (Veilleux & Tougas, 1989, p.493), males' reactions are likely to be individual-oriented; they may resent females for getting a better deal in job applications, or they may

74

lower their expectations about their own future employment prospects (Crosby & Clayton, 1990).

With regard to females who are the beneficiaries of the preferential treatment, the present findings suggest that females experienced feelings of discontent when they perceived that males were disadvantaged by sex-based selection. Such feelings of deprivation on behalf of others may have positive behavioral consequences for inequities in society. In two recent studies, it was found that when men experienced feelings of deprivation on behalf of women, they were more committed to the promotion of women's welfare (Tougas, Dube, & Veilleux, 1987; Veilleux & Tougas, 1989).

In the context of gender-based selection, one possible behavioral consequence of females' feelings of discontent (on behalf of men) could be that these women would also oppose gender-based preferential treatment in selection. Furthermore, research could also ascertain whether the reported negative effects of gender-based selection on women's self evaluations (e.g., Heilman et.al., 1987; Heilman et al, 1991) and on their job commitment and satisfaction (Chacko, 1982) are related to their feelings of discontent on behalf of men. Women might feel "guilty" of the unjust privileges they enjoy in the sense that they feel responsible for the disadvantages suffered by men. These negative emotions might then adversely affect their job-related evaluations and satisfaction.

6 Effect of justification on outcome fairness perceptions about preferential selection

The available evidence on outcome fairness judgements about preferential selection, both gender- and ethnicity-based, has been consistent in showing that such a selection practice is perceived as unfair. However, Crosby and Blanchard (1989) recently pointed out that although affirmative action programs may appear to jeopardize fairness and effectiveness,..... (these programs) seek to strengthen, and not to undermine, a just and smoothly organized society........ (and to) promote both true equity and effectiveness" (p.6) Because of the significant and far-reaching consequences that preferential selection may have on the workforce (e.g., Hoyt, 1989; Leonard, 1989; Sullivan, 1989) and on society (e.g., Bell, 1989; Garcia, 1989), people's perceptions about the justice of the program deserve more attention. The issue at stake appears to be the design of an effective preferential program that can achieve the goal of social justice and at the same time, be perceived as fair (Blanchard, 1989; Crosby & Clayton, 1991). Recent research on the effect of the provision of justifications on the reduction of perceived injustice is relevant to the pursuit of a preferential selection program that could be seen as fair.

Bies (1987a) argued that perceptions of outcome justice are the result of an argumentation or persuasion process. In the case of an unfair outcome, people's perceptions of injustice would be significantly reduced if adequate explanations are given for the decision making process leading to the outcome. In accounting for this "justification-reducing-injustice" effect, Tyler and Bies (1990) put forward two reasons: First, the information given in the justification may provide evidence that the unfavorable decision was indeed made after careful and thorough considerations by the decision maker. Second, the fact that the decision maker is willing to explain the reasons for the decision may in itself create the impression that the decision maker cares and hence can be trusted.

Several studies have reported the positive effect of justification on fairness perceptions. In a recruiting study, Bies and Shapiro (1988) provided a justification by informing the rejected job candidates that the reason for their rejection was because the company had entered into a phase of financial depression, hence a hiring freeze was imposed by top management. The results showed that such a justification significantly reduced perceptions of injustice. In a worker layoff context, it has been found that when management provided adequate accounts for the layoff, the layoff decision was perceived as less unfair (Brockner, 1990; Brockner, et al., 1990; Konovsky & Folger, 1991; Rousseau & Anton, 1988). In a pay cuts context, Greenberg (1990b) found that compared with no provision of justification, when the reasons for the pay cuts were provided in a "honest and caring " manner, employees perceived the pay cut decision as less unfair. A similar justification effect has been reported in a laboratory study involving a competitive game (Folger, Rosenfield & Robinson, 1983) and in other studies on management decisions (e.g., Folger & Bies, 1989; Tyler & Bies, 1990).

Bies further made the distinction between an ideological account and a causal account in justifying an unfavorable outcome or action (Bies, 1987a). The former provides justification for an action by invoking value-laden "superordinate goals" based on ethical or moral reasoning; the latter refers to an excuse aiming at lessening the responsibility of the actor or "harmdoer". In the context of preferential selection, the recruiting organization could explain its decision by providing candidates with the justifications put forward by proponents of preferential selection, namely, to correct past ills, to promote fair employment opportunities, and to utilize female talents (an "ethical justification"). Alternatively, the organization could claim that such decisions have to be made because they are required by existing legislative policies (a "legislative justification"). In Bies' terms, the former would constitute an ideological account and the latter, a causal account. Since research evidence on perceptions of outcome justice is convergent in showing that both ideological and causal accounts could reduce feelings of injustice, it is expected that preferential selection would be perceived as fairer when either an ethical or a legislation justification is given, than when no justification is provided.

77

Such an assumption is tested with reference to ethnicity-based selection in study 8, and gender-based selection in study 9 using a student sample and study 10 with a managerial sample. The same design applies to all three studies.

Design of the Studies

The hypothetical selection cases designed for study 6 in the evaluation of outcome fairness for gender-based and ethnicity-based selections are used in the present three studies. In order to examine the effect of justifications, a between-subjects design was used. There were three conditions of justification: "ethical justification", "legislative justification" and "no justification".

Subjects receiving the *ethical justification* were given this information after the hypothetical selection case:

"In justifying the decision, the personnel department wrote in the letter to all rejected candidates, that the firm has been concerned with the very small number of women (or "ethnic minorities" in the ethnicity-based selection case) currently working as computer programmers. Because historically females (or ethnic minorities) have been disadvantaged, the firm is interested in correcting such past ills. The firm is also committed to promote a fair distribution of employment opportunities as well as to broaden the overall talent pool by actively seeking qualified female (or ethnic minority) employees. The decision to appoint Sarah S. (or Fu-Tuk) was primarily due to the fact that she was the highest scoring female (or ethnic minority) candidate."

Subjects receiving the *legislative justification* were given this information:

"In justifying the decision, the personnel department wrote in the letter to all rejected candidates, that in recent years there has been an increasing number of female (or ethnic minority) graduates majoring in computer programming or related fields. Equal employment legislation stipulates that female (or ethnic minority) candidates be given equal employment opportunities without discrimination. The firm therefore feels obliged to actively seek qualified female (or ethnic minority) programmers to join its staff. The decision to offer the position to Sarah S. (or Fu-Tuk) was primarily due to the fact that she was the highest scoring female (or ethnic minority) candidate."

Subjects under the *no justification* condition were given no information after the hypothetical selection case.

In evaluating the case, respondents in studies 8 and 9 were

required to go through the same 11 items used in study 6, whereas respondents in study 10 answered the same 18 questions used in study 7. The additional items were measures of the deprivation construct (i.e., deserving, wanting, deprivation and discontent).

Manipulation checks were obtained from student subjects in study 9. All respondents receiving either form of the justification rated two additional items: (1) the extent to which the given justification reflects an *ethical consideration*, and (2) the extent to which the given justification reflects a *legislative policy*. Subjects receiving the ethical justification gave it a mean rating of 8.94 for reflecting an ethical consideration and a mean of 3.22 as reflecting a legislative policy, $t(318) = 12.92$, $p<.01$. The means for respondents receiving a legislative justification were 4.20 and 9.11 respectively, $t(316) = 10.98$, $p<.01$. The manipulations of justification therefore were perceived as intended.

Subjects and Results of Study 8

Study 8 deals with the justification effect on outcome fairness perceptions about ethnicity-based selection. The subject sample consisted of the same 240 overseas Asian students and 216 European students evaluating the ethnicity-based selection case in study 6. These subjects were randomly assigned to one of the three justification conditions. There were 80 Asian and 72 European students in each condition.

In data analyses, five scores (outcome fairness, appointee fairness, performance effectiveness, future expectation and repetition of appointment) were obtained for each respondent. Table 12 presents the mean ratings by justification conditions.

For European respondents, results of the analysis of variance showed that outcome fairness ratings were significantly affected by the provision of justification, $F(2,199) = 5.66$, $p<.01$. The cell means were 4.42 (no justification), 3.96 (ethical justification) and 3.43 (legislative justification). This indicates that when no justification was given, ethnicity-based selection decisions were considered as the least unfair; when legislation was given as a justification, the same decision was considered as more unfair. For Asian respondents, justification failed to have an effect on outcome fairness ratings, $F(2,224) =.46$.

Results of other four dependent variables showed that justification had little impact on all but one of these variables: For Asian respondents, justification significantly affected performance effectiveness ratings, $F(2,224) = 3.27$, $p<.05$. This indicates that

79

Table 12
Mean ratings: Study 8

Subject sample	Justification	Dependent Variables: Outcome fairness	Appointee fairness	Performance effectiveness	Future expectation	Repetition of appointment
Europeans	No	4.42	7.08	6.05	5.00	4.33
	Ethical	3.96	6.80	5.96	4.22	4.17
	Legislative	3.43	6.91	5.36	4.36	3.86
Asians	No	4.77	7.05	6.48	5.94	5.45
	Ethical	4.51	6.93	5.84	5.27	5.17
	Legislative	4.56	6.45	6.01	5.20	5.17

Asians judged the minority appointee's future job performance as more effective when no justification was given, than when either of the two justifications was provided.

Subjects and Results of Study 9

Study 9 examines the justification effect on outcome fairness perceptions about gender-based selection. The sample consisted of the same 480 (240 male and 240 female) students evaluating the gender-based selection case in study 6. Altogether 80 males and 80 females were randomly assigned to each of the three justification conditions.

Table 13 presents the mean ratings for the five dependent measures by justifications. For male respondents, justification had a significant effect on outcome fairness, $F(2, 456) = 10.60$, $p < .01$, indicating that when no justification was given, gender-based selection was perceived as the least unfair than when either justification was provided.

For female respondents, justification also had a significant effect on outcome fairness ratings, $F(2, 456) = 4.84$, $p < .01$, indicating that gender-based selection was perceived as significantly more unfair when either justification was provided. The finding therefore is consistent with that of male respondents.

Regarding the other four dependent variables, justification had significant effects on male respondents' ratings of appointee fairness, $F(2, 456) = 5.18$, $p < .01$; and performance effectiveness, $F(2, 456) = 3.99$, $p < .05$. These results indicate that when no justification was provided, the ratings were more favorable than when either justification was given.

Subjects and Results of Study 10

Using a managerial sample, study 10 examines the justification effect on outcome fairness perceptions about gender-based selection. In addition, the effect of justification on feelings of deprivation and discontent due to such a selection was also explored.

The sample consisted of the same 281 (185 male and 96 female) managerial professionals in study 7. These respondents were randomly assigned to one of the three justification conditions. For each respondent, eight scores were obtained: outcome fairness, deserving, wanting, deprivation, discontent, appointee performance, future expectations, and repetition of appointment. Table 14 presents the mean ratings for the eight measures. Because

81

Table 13
Mean ratings: Study 9

Subject sample	Justification	Dependent Variables				
		Outcome fairness	Appointee fairness	Performance effectiveness	Future expectation	Repetition of appointment
Males	No	4.15	7.56	6.08	4.99	4.45
	Ethical	3.06	6.70	5.98	4.19	4.13
	Legislative	2.57	6.69	5.40	4.85	4.33
Females	No	4.21	7.30	6.50	4.99	4.76
	Ethical	3.64	6.84	6.56	5.08	4.44
	Legislative	3.38	7.04	6.49	5.54	4.70

Table 14
Mean ratings: Study 10

Justification	Outcome fairness	Deserving	Wanting	Deprivation	Discontent	Appointee performance	Future expectation	Repetition of appointment
No	4.05	6.73	7.24	7.56	7.79	6.35	5.81	4.43
Ethical	2.51	7.56	7.32	8.31	8.09	6.70	6.10	3.93
Legislative	2.30	7.40	6.75	8.08	8.19	6.52	6.52	3.87

Dependent Variables

of the small number of female respondents in each justification condition, data analyses were carried out on aggregated data based on the entire sample.

The effect of justification was significant for outcome fairness ratings, $F(2, 269) = 18.04$, $p<.01$. An examination of the cell means revealed that when no justification was given, professionals perceived gender-based selection outcomes as the least unfair. When either justification was provided, the same selection outcome was perceived as more unfair. A similar trend was also observed for three of the four dependent variables measuring the deprivation construct. For the variable deserving, $F(2,269)=5.57$, $p<.05$; wanting, $F(2,269)=3.84$, $p<.05$; and deprivation, $F(2,269) = 6.39$, $p<.01$. An examination of the cell means showed that consistent for all three variables, the provision of justifications had a worsening effect in that the rejected candidate was perceived as being more deserving and more eager to get the job as well as feeling more deprived of a better outcome. However, justification had no significant effect on any of the other three dependent variables of appointee performance, future expectation and repetition of appointment.

Effect of Justification on Perceptions of Fairness and Emotions of Deprivation

In terms of outcome fairness perceptions about preferential selection, consistent findings are obtained from these three studies: as compared with the condition of no justification, preferential selection outcomes were perceived as more unfair when either an ethical or a legislative justification was provided. In other words, the provision of either form of justification further exacerbated perceptions of injustice. This finding is evident in European respondents' evaluations of ethnicity-based selection in study 8, in both male and female students' evaluations of gender-based selection in study 9, and in managerial professionals' perceptions of gender-based selection in study 10. Furthermore, justification had a similar worsening effect on professionals' emotional reactions to gender-based selection.

These results, although internally consistent, are different from research findings to date suggesting that the provision of justification has a fairness-enhancing effect on justice perceptions. Also in a recruiting context, Bies and Shapiro (1988) reported a significant reduction in the level of perceived injustice when a justification was provided to the rejected job candidate. There are several likely interpretations for the inconsistency between the present findings and those of Bies and Shapiro's (1988): First, unlike in Bies and Shapiro study, the selection cases used in the present studies were likely to be seen as reflecting an existing social policy. In other words, the decision in Bies and Shapiro study was seen as unjust with regard to one individual candidate; whereas in this study the decision was perhaps seen as unjust with reference to all males or all Europeans (or all candidates who are males or Europeans). It seems that any attempt to justify a more widespread and lasting unfair outcome would trigger off greater resistance or "psychological reactance" (Brehm, 1966). The provision of either form of justification in the present studies thus exacerbated feelings of injustice.

While the first interpretation focused on the severity of consequence (i.e., the number of potential victims), the second interpretation is that in the present studies, but not in that of Bies and Shapiro, the issue of sex- or race-based discrimination was at stake. Social psychological research has shown that cognitions and attitudes associated with sex or racial discrimination are schema-driven and hence are resilient (e.g., Stephan, 1985). Any justification would consequently be met with further resistance.

The third interpretation concerns whether a "winner" is present in the selection cases. In Bies and Shapiro study, no candidate was offered the job. In the present studies the selection cases always involved a job offer to the minority candidate (i.e., the winner).The presence of such a winner referent is significant for judgements of justice. Central to most outcome justice theories (e.g., equity and relative deprivation theories) are the referent comparison process and the relative nature of fairness judgements. In the absence of a winner referent, the allocation appears to have left everyone "in the same boat". However, in the presence of such a referent, the comparison process would be more likely to exacerbate feelings of injustice when it was clear that the winner was not the most qualified or merited.

The fourth possible interpretation concerns the "situational vs. dispositional" nature of the justification. In their recruitment study, Bies and Shapiro (1988) used a situational justification (i.e, financial depression of the company) as an explanation for not making an appointment. In the present studies, both the ethical and legislation justifications involved a personal or dispositional element (i.e., the candidate's gender or ethnic origin). Attribution research has shown that "actors" tended to attribute own failures to situational , rather than personal factors (e.g., Jones & Nisbett, 1972).

Respondents in these studies are likely to assume the role of an actor, that is, they may empathize with the rejected candidate through gender or ethnic membership identities (Tajfel, 1982). Compared with situational reasons, causal explanations involving personal factors might induce feelings of dissonance or uneasiness (e.g., Festinger,1954), hence the decision would be perceived as more unfair.

The fifth possible interpretation concerns whether respondents in the no-justification conditions attempted to speculate on the reasons for the selection outcome themselves. In doing so, they are likely to have come up with explanations that are more convincing than either the ethical or legislative justification provided by the experimenter. The higher fairness ratings observed under the no-justification conditions could therefore be a result of such self-induced and more persuasive justifications.

With specific reference to ethnicity-based preferential selection, one other possible interpretation concerns the issue of minority employment. History is replete with incidents of racial tension due to "foreigners" stealing away employment opportunities from "locals". Any attempt in justifying such outcomes might inevitably be met with "psychological reactance" (Brehm, 1966). This line of reasoning would further predict that the use of a hard line approach in implementing preferential selection (e.g., through legislation) would induce greater resistance than an approach based on grounds of humanity. This is consistent with the present finding of study 8 showing that ethnicity-based selection outcomes were seen by Europeans, as even more unfair under the condition of legislation justification than the ethical justification condition.

In the light of the finding of study 10 showing that justifications for gender-based selections not only exacerbated perceptions of injustice, but also intensified aversive emotional reactions towards the program, it appears reasonable to assume that when a perceived injustice was accompanied by strong emotions, any attempts to give justification to the injustice would tend to make the matter worse. Given this, earlier studies showing a reduction in perceived injustice following the provision of justification may have involved issues that are not as controversial or emotionally provoking as gender- or race-based preferential treatment in selection.

7 Summary of findings and other potential applications of justice notions to selection fairness research

This book advocates an organizational justice approach to selection fairness research. It is argued that current organizational justice theories provide a thorough and integrative conceptual framework for fairness issues in organizational settings and that research into the fairness of personnel selection practices would benefit in theory and practice from taking such a perspective.

The book has attempted to identify specific issues of fairness in selection to which organizational justice theories could be fruitfully applied. In doing so, the book has reported the available but limited empirical research taking the proposed approach.

Summary of Proposed Applications and Research Findings

It has been proposed that selection fairness research can benefit from the approach taking either a procedural justice or outcome justice perspective.

(A) Applying Procedural Justice Notions to Selection

Relevant procedural justice notions are useful in the identification of key determinants of fair selection procedures, and in the examination of possible behavioral consequences of candidates' fairness perceptions about the selection procedures.

Identifying Determinants of Fair Selection Procedures

Leventhal at al's (1980) allocation preference theory provides an ideal theoretical framework for research aiming at identifying determinants of fair procedures. Adopting the open-ended question and factorial analysis method used by Greenberg (1986a) in identifying fair procedures of performance appraisal, Studies 1, 2 and 3 examined the underlying determinants of a fair selection practice for both managerial and entry level positions. For managerial selection, several factors were identified as the key fairness factors: "honest and thorough communication", "choice of selectors", "voice and information soliciting", "open objective competition", "consistency and ethicality"," bias avoidance", and "the use of job-relevant criteria". These factors are in close agreement with the principles of procedural justice proposed by the allocation preference theory. Similar fairness factors were also identified for entry-level selections, indicating that the principles of fair procedures specified in the allocation preference theory are applicable to both managerial and entry-level selections (Singer, 1990a).

Consequences of Fairness Perceptions about Selection Procedures

In recent selection literature, several theorists have argued that because the selection process represents the initial phase of a continuing social interaction process between the recruiting organization and the applicant, selection research should focus more on the longer-term impact of the selection process on applicants' post-selection attitudes and behavior (e.g., Herriot, 1989; Robertson & Smith, 1989; Taylor & Bergmann, 1987). In the procedural justice literature, Lind and Tyler (1988) have called for research into possible behavioral consequences of individuals' perceptions of procedural fairness. In this context, study 4 examined the effects of candidates' fairness perceptions about the selection procedures on their later job attitudes. Specifically, the effects of fairness perceptions about process-control procedures and decision-control procedures were compared. In Thibaut and Walker's (1978) original theory, decision-control was conceptualised as the more decisive means in assuring fair outcomes. Individuals resort to rely on process controls when direct control over final decisions was not possible. Process- control are therefore indirect means in assuring the fairness of the final outcome. It was found that fairness perceptions about process-control procedures were predictive of candidates' post-entry organizational commitment, work satisfaction as well as their perceptions of overall organizational effectiveness. However, candidates' fairness perceptions about decision-control procedures had no impact on these job attitudes (Singer, 1992a).

(B) Applying Outcome Justice Notion to Preferential Selection

Outcome Fairness Perceptions About Preferential Selection

It is argued that outcome justice notions are most applicable to issues of preferential selection. Although consideration of outcome justice is fundamental to preferential selection and that theorists have argued for (e.g., America, 1986) and against (e.g., Newton, 1973) the fairness of preferential treatment in selection, only limited empirical research has addressed this issue. These studies have identified a number of factors having a significant effect on outcome fairness judgements about preferential selection:

1. Merit Discrepancy It has been found that fairness perceptions about preferential selection are significantly affected by the size of discrepancy in merit between the rejected but more merited majority candidate and the minority appointee; the greater the discrepancy, the more unfair the decision was judged. This merit discrepancy effect has been consistently observed for both gender-based and ethnicity-based preferential selection in either a within-subjects or between-subjects design (Studies 5,6, and 7) (Singer, 1990b; 1992b; 1992c).

2. Objective vs. Subjective Perspective of the Perceiver Although justice theorists have argued for the importance of the rules of "veil of ignorance" (Rawls, 1971) and "impartiality" (Soltan, 1987) in judgements of justice, there is evidence suggesting that ethnicity-based preferential selection is judged as unfair, irrespective of whether respondents taking a subjective participant perspective or an objective bystander's perspective (Singer, 1992b). Furthermore, fairness judgements about gender-based selection outcomes appear comparable between findings of study using a "self-reporting" approach (a subjective perspective) (Veilleux & Tougas, 1989) and that using a hypothetical "scenario" approach (an objective perspective) (Studies 6 and 7).

3. Victim vs. Beneficiary Status of the Perceiver   While the potential victims of either gender-based (i.e., males) or ethnicity-based (i.e., whites) selections consistently perceived such selection outcomes as unjust (Heilman et al, 1991; Veilleux & Tougas, 1989), findings on fairness perceptions of the beneficiaries (females for gender-based selections and ethnic minorities for ethnicity-based selections) appear to be influenced by the type of preferential treatment. For gender-based selections, Study 6 shows that females had similar fairness perceptions to those of males. For ethnicity-based selections, ethnic minorities' fairness perceptions appear to be influenced by merit discrepancy: When merit discrepancy was small, the beneficiaries did not seem to consider the preferential treatment as unfair (Study 6).

4. Individual Differences   While several studies have examined individual differences in justice judgements (e.g., Mayor, Bylsma & Cozzarelli, 1989; Sweeney, McFarlin & Cotton, 1991), only two studies have been carried out with reference to preferential selection. Tougas, Beaton and Veilleux (1991) found that while most women opposed preferential selection, women who had experienced gender-related discriminations in their work, were supportive of gender-based selection.   Based on Pettigrew's (1958) theory of category width, Singer (1990c) hypothesised that narrow categorisers, being more sensitive to differences among stimuli, would be more influenced by the size of merit discrepancies between candidates. They are therefore more likely to perceive preferential selection as unfair. However, no significant difference in perceived fairness was found on the individual differences dimension of category width.   Future research could ascertain whether fairness perceptions about preferential selection are likely to be influenced by differences in individuals' social political or ethical beliefs.

5. the Provision of Justification   In arguing that the provision of justifications could significantly reduce victim's feelings of injustice, Bies (1987a) made the distinction between an ideological account and a causal account in justifying an unfavourable outcome or action. In the context of preferential selection, It was found that the provision of either an "ethical" (i.e., ideological) or a "legislative" (i.e., causal) justification for the preferential treatment of the candidates, rather than reducing perceptions of injustice , further exacerbated the perceived injustice (Studies 8, 9, and 10)

(Singer, 1990b; 1992c).

   6. "Framing" Effect   People's *opinions* on preferential selection
have been shown to be subject to the framing effect (e.g., Brunner,
1986; Tversky & Kahneman, 1981). Kinder and Sanders (1990)
showed that when preferential selection is framed as "reverse
discrimination", as opposed to "unfair advantage", there was a
further decrease in the level of people's approval for the program.
Future research could ascertain whether individuals' *fairness
perceptions* about preferential selection are also similarly affected by
such a framing effect.

Consequences of Outcome Fairness Perceptions on Behavior

Evidence so far is convergent in showing that preferential selection
results in perceptions of injustice. It is argued that the most
relevant theory in interpreting these findings appears to be the
outcome justice theory of relative deprivation. Because relative
deprivation theory has provisions for group comparisons in terms
of the notion of group or fraternal deprivation, the theory could
directly address the issue of group inequity as a result of preferential
treatment. Furthermore, because the theory has postulated on
behavioral consequences of deprivation, the theory could allow the
examination of possible behavioral reactions to preferential
selection.
   To this end, study 7 has demonstrated directly that gender-based
selection also induced feelings of deprivation and discontent
among the potentially disadvantaged group (i.e., males). A similar
finding was reported by Veilleux and Tougas (1989). These studies
therefore have paved the way for further application of the theory
to relevant behavioral consequences of feelings of deprivation.
Several directions for future research taking this line of enquiry are
proposed in Chapter five.

Other Potential Applications of Justice Notions to Selection Fairness Research

In addition to the proposed application of outcome justice and
procedural justice notions, selection research could further benefit
from the application of other recently developed justice concepts.
More specifically, the concept of interactional justice is applicable to

9 1

selection interview research. Research on the justification effect and the scope of justice effect is relevant to fairness issues in preferential selection. Finally, achieving justice in selection could constitute a significant subfield in the psychology of improving justice, a concept recently advocated by Cook (1990).

Interactional Justice in Selection Interviews

Selection interview research has so far explicitly or implicitly focused on two issues of interview decision making: First, the moving away from the individual-orientation, typically characterises traditional unstructured interviews, to one involving the use of consistent rules for each and every individual candidate. Second, the correction of biases or discrimination against any individual candidate because of his/her minority group membership status. Both issues concern justice: In the context of Leventhal et al's (1980) six principles of procedural justice, the former concerns the principle of consistency in rules, and the latter concerns the principle of bias avoidance. Cumulative research efforts have identified means to achieve these two aspects of justice in selection interview decisions:

(1) The use of highly structured interviews to ensure consistency. The development of structured interviews, situational interviews and the PBDI (reviewed in Chapter 3) has contributed to the standardization of interview content. This has therefore made possible the application of consistent rules to individual candidate in interviews.

(2) The use of information exposure about successful minority candidate to eliminate interview biases due to minority status. Heilman and Martell (1986) found that the gender-bias effect could be eliminated by the provision of repeated information about successful women to interviewers prior to the interviews. Using a similar method of repeated information exposure, Singer and Sewell (1989) attempted to reduce the age-bias effect in interview decision making. The study, while unsuccessful in eliminating age-bias effect, have shed light on the importance of the content of the information used. The study could therefore contribute to the design of future research adopting the information exposure method in rectifying interview biases.

In the entire selection process, interviews provide an unique opportunity for face-to-face interactions between recruiters and job candidates. However, because the traditional focus of interview research has been on the aforementioned issues, the dynamic nature of the two-way interactional processes has been largely overlooked. In the context of justice theories, the notion of interactional justice appears particularly relevant to the recruiter-candidate exchange process during interviews. Future research could first, identify key criteria for fair recruiter-candidate interactions in interviews, and second, examine the impact of interactional justice on candidates' post-interview reactions and post-entry attitudes and behavior.

Justification Effects in Preferential Selection

Although evidence so far suggests that the provision of justification reduces perceptions of injustice about a variety of managerial decisions (e.g., Brockner, 1990; Greenberg, 1990; Tyler & Bies, 1990), in the context of preferential selection, however, the provision of justification for preferential selection decisions has been found to further exacerbate feelings of injustice (Studies 8, 9 and 10). There are a number of likely reasons for the observed inconsistency in the justification effect. These include the presence or absence of a winner referent, the dispositional vs. situational nature of the justification, and the extent to which psychological reactance is generated by the justifications provided. Future research should examine the underlying mechanism of the justification effect with the aim of identifying moderator factors in the justification and selection fairness relationship. As Crosby and Clayton (1990) point out that in order to avoid the negative effects of affirmative action programs on expectancies and behavior, such programs "must be, and also must appear to be, fair" (p.73). Research findings on how preferential selection outcomes could be perceived as fairer through the use of justifications would therefore have practical significance for the successful implementation of such programs.

Scope of Justice and Selection Fairness

Research on the scope of justice to date suggests that an individual's scope of justice has a significant effect on his/her judgement of justice (Tyler & Lind, 1990). Logically, this scope of justice effect would extend to the person's judgement of the fairness of preferential selection outcomes. It is likely that the strength of the social identity (Tajfel, 1982; Tajfel & Turner, 1979) an individual ascribes to his/her own gender or ethnic group would determine the person's scope of justice and hence influence the fairness judgements of preferential selection outcomes. It is equally likely that the strength of empathy an individual feels towards the "outgroups" may be one other such determinant. Selection fairness research could explore first, the underlying determinants of an individual's scope of justice (e.g., identification with ingroups and/or empathy towards outgroups); and second, how these determinants interact in determining the person's fairness judgement of preferential selection outcomes. The findings could contribute not only to the understanding of the justice of preferential selection, but to the successful planning or implementation of the program.

Cook's Notion of the Psychology of Improving Justice and Selection Fairness

The notion of improving justice is relevant to all social issues including the allocation of employment opportunities. It is specifically applicable to the issue of minority employment and preferential selection. While it is generally agreed that social injustice does exist in this regard and that one of the main goals of society is to eliminate all forms of inequality in order to achieve justice in employment conditions, there is much less agreement on the exact means in achieving such a goal. For instance, early equity theorists argued for the necessity of a direct redistribution of economic and social power between the majority and minorities in society in order to bring about social justice (e.g., Walster & Walster, 1975). Several recent justice theorists echo a similar view in advocating the implementation of affirmative action policies (e.g., Crosby & Clayton, 1990).

Based on the extensive social psychological literature on intergroup relations, Cook (1990) however recently argues for an indirect means in achieving social equality through the promoting of liking and respect for, and ultimately the extending of the scope of justice to subordinate social groups. Given the substantial empirical evidence on the opposition and reactance to preferential selection policies (e.g., Kinder & Sanders, 1990; Nascote, 1989; Tougas & Veilleux, 1989), Cook's indirect approach to improving social justice may indeed be the most promising means in attenuating perceptions of injustice and opposition to preferential selection. Cast in this context, the evaluations of such policies would have to go beyond the outcome, procedural and interactional justice issues , and to include considerations of compensatory, retribution and restitution justice issues (e.g., Clayton & Tangri, 1989; Groarke, 1990).

94

References

Adams, J.S. (1965). Inequity in social exchange. In L. Berkowitz (Ed.), *Advances in experimental social psychology* (vol.2), p.267- 299. New York: Academic Press.

Alexander, S., & Ruderman, M. (1987). The role of procedural and distributive justice in organizational behavior. *Social Justice Research*, 1, 117-198.

Ambrose, M.L., Harland, L.K., & Kulik, C.T. (1991). Influence of social comparison on perceptions of organizational fairness. *Journal of Applied Psychology*, 76, 239-246.

America, R.F. (1986). Affirmative action and redistributive ethics. *Journal of Business Ethics*, 5, 73-77.

Arvey, R.D. (1979). Unfair discrimination in the employment interview: Legal and psychological aspects. *Psychological Bulletin*, 86, 736-765.

Arvey, R.D. (1986). General ability in employment : A discussion. *Journal of Vocational Behavior*, 29, 415-420.

Arvey, R.D., & Campion, J.E. (1982). The employment interview: A summary and review of recent research. *Personnel Psychology*, 35, 281-322.

Arvey, R.D., Miller, H.E., Gould, R., & Burch, P. (1987). Interview validity for selecting sales clerks. *Personnel Psychology*, 40, 1-12.

Ash, P., Baehr, M.E., Joy, D.S., & Orban, J.A. (1988). *Applied Psychology: An International Review*, 37, 351-362.

Barr, S.H., & Hitt, M.A. (1986). A comparison of selection decision models in manager versus student samples. *Personnel Psychology*, 39, 599-617.

Barrett-Howard, E., & Tyler, T.R. (1986). Procedural justice as a criterion in allocation decisions. *Journal of Personality and Social Psychology*, 50, 296-304.

Barrick, M.R., & Mount, M.K. (1991). The big five personality dimensions and job performance: A meta-analysis. *Personnel Psychology*, 44, 1-26.

Bartlett, C.J., Bobko, P., Mosier, S.B., & Hannan, R. (1978). Testing for fairness with a moderated multiple regression strategy: An alternative to differential analysis. *Personnel Psychology*, 31, 233-241.

Becker, T.E., & Klimoski, R.J. (1989). A field study of the relationship between the organizational feedback environment and performance. *Personnel Psychology*, 42, 343-358.

Bell, D. (1989). The effects of affirmative action on make female relationships among African Americans. *Sex Roles*, 21, 13-24.

Bies, R.J. (1986, August). Identifying principles of interactional justice: The case of corporate recruiting. In R.J. Bies (chair), *Moving beyond equity theory: New directions in research in justice in organizations.* Symposium conducted at the annual meeting of the Academy of Management, Chicago.

Bies, R.J. (1987a). The predicament of injustice: The management of moral outrage. In L.L. Cummings & B.M. Staw (Eds.), *Research in organizational behavior* (Vol. 9), p.289-319. Greenwich, CT: JAI Press.

Bies, R.J. (1987b). Beyond voice: The influence of decision-maker justification and sincerity on procedural fairness judgments. *Representative Research in Social Psychology*, 17, 3-14.

Bies, R.J., & Moag, J.S. (1986). Interactional justice: Communication criteria of fairness. In R.J. Lewicki, B.H. Sheppard, & M.H. Bazerman (Eds.), *Research on negotiation in organizations* (pp. 43-55). Greenwich, CT: JAI Press.

Bies, R.J., & Shapiro, D.L. (1988). Voice and justification: Their influence on procedural fairness judgments. *Academy of Management Journal*, 31, 676-685.

Blanchard, F.A. (1989). Effective affirmative action programs. In F.A. Blanchard & F. Crosby (Eds.), *Affirmative action in perspective* (pp.193-208). New York: Springer-Verlag.

Blinkhorn, S., & Johnson, C. (1990). The insignificance of personality testing. *Nature*, 348, 671-672.

Boehm, V.R. (1977). Differential prediction: A methodological artifact? *Journal of Applied Psychology*, 62, 146-154.

Bolick, C. (1988). Legal and policy aspects of testing. *Journal of*

Vocational Behavior, 33, 320-330.

Brehm, J. W. (1966). *A theory of Psychological reactance.* New York: Academic Press.

Brockner, J. (1990). Scope of justice in the workplace: How survivors react to co-worker layoffs. *Journal of Social Issues, 46,* 95-106.

Brockner, J., DeWitt, R., Grover, S., & Reed, T. (1990). When it is especially important to explain why: Factors affecting the relationship between managers' explanations of a layoff and survivors' reactions to the layoff. *Journal of Experimental Social Psychology, 26,* 389-407.

Bruner, J. (1986). *Actual milnds, possible worlds.* Cambridge, MA: Harvard University Press.

Callender, J.C., & Osburn, H.G. (1980). Development and test of a new model of validity generalization. *Journal of Applied Psychology, 65,* 543-558.

Campbell, D.T., & Stanley, J.C. (1967). *Experimental and quasi-experimental designs for research.* Chicago: Rand McNally.

Campbell, J.P., & Pritchard, R.A. (1976). Motivation theory in industrial and organizational psychology, In M.D. Dunnette (Ed.), *Handbook of industrial and organizational psychology* (pp.63-130). Chicago: Rand McNally.

Campion, J.E., & Arvey, R.D. (1989). Unfair discrimination in the employment interview. In R.W. Eder & G.R. Ferris (Eds.), *The employment interview.* London: Sage.

Campion, M.A., Pursell, E.D., & Brown, B.K. (1988). Structured interviewing: Raising the psychometric properties of the employment interview. *Personnel Psychology, 41,* 25-42.

Cascio, W.F. (1982). *Costing human resources: The financial impact of behavior in organizations.* Boston, Mass: Kent.

Cascio, W.F. (1987). *Applied psychology in personnel management* (3rd ed.). Englewood Cliffs, N.J.: Prentice-Hall.

Cascio, W.F. (1991). *Applied psychology in personnel management* (4th ed.) Englewood Cliffs: N.J.: Prentice-Hall.

Chacko, T.I. (1982). Women and equal employment opportunity: Some unintended effects. *Journal of Applied Psychology, 67,* 119-123.

Chusmir, L.H., & Mills, J (1989). Gender differences in conflict resolution styles of managers: At work and at home. *Sex Roles, 20,* 149-163.

Clayton, S.D., & Tangri, S.S. (1989). The justice of affirmative action. In F.A. Blanchard & F.C. Crosby (Eds). *Affirmative action in perspective.* New York: Springer-Verlag.

97

Cleary, T. A. (1968). Test bias: Prediction of grades of negro and white students in integrated colleges. *Journal of Educational Measurement*, 5, 115-124.

Cleveland, J.N., Festa, R.M., & Montegomery, L (1988). Applicant pool composition and job perception: Impact on decisions regarding an older applicant. *Journal of Vocational Behavior*, 32, 112-125.

Cohen, R.L. (1989). Fabrications of justice. Social Justice Research, 3, 31-46.

→Cole, N.S. (1973). Bias in selection. *Journal of Educational Measurement*, 10, 237-255.

Cook, S.W. (1990). Toward a psychology of improving justice: Research on extending the equality principle to victims of social injustice. *Journal of Social Issues*, 46, 147-161.

Cook, T.D., & Campbell, D.T. (1976). *Quasi-experimentation: Design and analysis issues for field settings*. Boston: Houghton Mifflin.

Cronbach, L.J., & Schaeffer, G.A. (1981). *Extensions of personnel selection theory to aspects of minority hiring*. (Project report no. 81-A2). Palo Alto, CA: Stanford University.

Cronbach, L.J., Yalow, E., & Schaeffer, G.A. (1980). A mathematical structure for analyzing fairness in selection. *Personnel Psychology*, 33, 693-704.

→Cronshaw, S.F., & Wiesner, W.H. (1989). The validity of the employment interview: Models for research and practice.
→ In R.W. Eder & G. R. Ferris (Eds.), *The employment interview*. London: Sage.

Cropanzano, R., & Folger, R. (1989). Referent cognitions and task decision autonomy: Beyond equity theory. *Journal of Applied Psychology*, 74, 293-299.

Crosby, F. (1976). A model of egoistic relative deprivation. *Psychological Review*, 83, 85-113.

Crosby, F. (1982). *Relative deprivation and working women*. New York: Oxford University Press.

Crosby, F. (1984). Relative deprivation in organizational settings. In B.M. Staw & L.L. Cummings (Eds.), *Research in organizational behavior* (Vol. 6, pp. 51-93). Greenwich, CT: JAI Press.

Crosby, F., & Blanchard, F. (1989). Introduction: Affirmative action and the question of standards. In F. Blanchard & F. Crosby (Eds). *Affirmative action in perspective* (pp.3-7). New York: Springer-Verlag.

Crosby, F., & Clayton, S. (1990). Affirmative action and the issue of expectancies. *Journal of Social Issues*, 46, 61-79.

Darlington, R.B. (1971). Another look at cultural fairness. *Journal of Educational Measurement*, 8, 71-82.

Davies, J. (1959). A formal interpretation of the theory of relative deprivation. *Sociometry*, 22, 280-296.

deCarufel, A. (1986). Pay secrecy, social comparison and relative deprivation in organizations. In J.M. Olson, C.P. Herman & M.P. Zanna (Eds.), *Relative deprivation and social comparison: The Ontario Symposium* (Vol. 4), pp.181-199

Deutsch, M. (1985). *Distributive justice: A social-psychological perspective*. New Haven: Yale University Press.

Dickey-Bryant, L., Lautenschlager, G.L., Mendoza, J.L., & Abrahams, N. (1986). Facial attractiveness and its relation to occupational success. *Journal of Applied Psychology*, 71, 16-19.

Donaldson, T., & Werhane, P.H. (1983). *Ethical issues in business: A philosophical approach* (2nd Ed.). Englewood Cliffs, N.J.: Prentice-Hall.

Dornstein, M. (1989). The fairness judgements of received pay and their determinants. *Journal of Occupational Psychology*, 62, 287-299.

Eder, R.W., Buckley, M.R. (1988). The employment interview: An interactionist perspective. In G.R. Ferris & K.M. Rowland (Eds.), *Research in personnel and human resources management* (Vol. 6, pp. 75-107). Greenwich, CT: JAI Press.

Einhorn, H.J., & Bass, A.R. (1971). Methodological considerations relevant to discrimination in employment testing. *Psychological Bulletin*, 75, 261-269.

Eysenck, H.J. (1984). The effect of race on human abilities and mental test scores. In C.R. & R.T. Brown (Eds.), *Perspectives on bias in mental testing* (pp.249-292). New York: Plenum.

Ferris, G.R., Bergin, T.G., & Gilmore, D.C. (1986). Personality and ability predictors of training performance for flight attendants. *Group and Organizational Studies*, 11, 419-435.

Festinger, L. (1954). A theory of social comparison processes. *Human Relations*, 1, 117-149.

Fisher, C.D. (1984). Laboratory experiments. In T. S. Bateman & G.R. Ferris (Eds.), *Method and analysis in organizational research* (pp.169-185). Reston, VA: Prentice-Hall.

Fletcher, C. (1987). Candidate personality as an influence on selection interview assessment, *Applied Psychology: An International Review*, 36, 157-162.

99

Fletcher, C. (1991). Candidates' reactions to assessment centres and their outcomes: A longitudinal study. *Journal of Occupational Psychology, 64,* 117-127.

Folger, R. (1986a). Rethinking equity theory: A referent cognitions model In H.W. Bierhoff, R.L. Cohen & J. Greenberg (Eds.), *Justice in social relations.* (pp.145-162). New York: Plenum.

Folger, R. (1986b). A referent cognitions theory of relative deprivation. In J.M. Olson, C. P. Herman & M.P. Zanna (Eds.), *Social comparison and relative deprivation: The Ontario Symposium* (Vol. 4, pp.33-55). Hillsdale, N.J.: Erlbaum.

Folger, R. (1988). *Justice as dignity.* Paper presented at American Psychological Association meeting, Atlanta.

Folger, R., & Bies, R.J. (1989). Managerial responsibilities and procedural justice. *Employee Responsibilities and Rights Journal, 2,* 79-90.

Folger, R., & Greenberg, J (1985). Procedural justice: An interpretive analysis of personnel systems. In K. Rowland & G. Ferris (Eds.), *Research in personnel and human resources management* (Vol. 3), pp.141-183. Greenwich, CT:JAI Press.

Folger, R., & Konovsky, M.A. (1989). Effects of procedural and distributive justice on reactions to pay raise decisions. *Academy of Management Journal, 32,* 115-130.

Folger, R., Rosenfield, D., & Robinson, T. (1983). Relative deprivation and procedural justifications. *Journal of Personality and Social Psychology, 45,* 268-273.

Freytag, W.R. (1976). The validity of the oral board interview in police officer selection: A comparative analysis between minority group members and white males. Unpublished manuscript. Harrisburg: Pennsylvania State University, Applied Research Laboratory.

Fry, W.R., & Cheney, G. (1981, May). *Perceptions of procedural fairness as a function of distributive preference.* Paper presented at the meeting of the Midwestern Psychological Association, Detroit.

Fry, W.R., & Leventhal, G.S. (1979, March). Cross-situational procedural preferences: A comparison of allocation preferences and equity across different social settings. In A. Lind (Chair), *The psychology of procedural justice.* Symposium conducted at the meeting of the Southwestern Psychological Association, Washington, DC.

Fryxell, G.E., & Gordon, M.E. (1989). Workplace justice and job satisfaction as predictors of satisfaction with union and management. *Academy of Management Journal, 32,* 851-866.

Furby, L. (1986). Psychology and justice. In R.L. Cohen (Ed.), *Justice: Views from the social sciences* (pp.153-203). New York: Plenum.

Garcia, S.A. (1989). My sister's keeper: Negative effects of social welfare and affirmative action programs on black women. *Sex Roles, 21,* 25-43.

Gardner, H. (1983). *Frames of mind: The theory of multiple intelligence.* New York: Basic Books.

Garrett, T.M., & Klonoski, R.J. (1986). *Business ethics (2nd Ed.),* Englewood Cliffs, NJ: Prentice Hall.

Goldman, A.H. (1975). Limits to the justification of reverse discrimination. *Social Theory and Practice, 3,* 110-113.

Goldman, A.H. (1976). Affirmative action. Philosophy and Public Affairs, 5, 187.

Goodman, P.S., & Friedman, A. (1971). An examination of Adam's theory of inequity. *Administrative Science Quarterly, 16,* 271-288.

Gordon, R.A. (1984). The effect of accountability on age discrimination in the employment interview. *Dissertation Abstracts International, 45,* 3113.

Gordon, R.A., Rozelle, R.M., & Baxter, J.C. (1988). The effect of applicant age, job level, and accountability of the evaluation of job applicants. *Organizational Behavior and Human Decision Process, 41,* 20-33.

Gottfredson, L.S. (1986a). Societal consequences of the g factor in employment. *Journal of Vocational Behavior, 29,* 397-410.

Gottfredson, L.S. (1986b). The g factor in employment (Special issue). *Journal of Vocational Behavior, 29.*

Gottfredson, L.S. (1988). Reconsidering fairness: A matter of social and ethical priorities. *Journal of Vocational Behavior, 33,* 293-319.

Gottfredson, L.S., & Crouse, J. (1986). Validity versus utility of mental tests: Example of the SAT. *Journal of Vocational Behavior, 29,* 363-378.

Gottfredson, L.S., & Sharf, J.C. (1988). Fairness in employment testing (Special issue). *Journal of Vocational Behavior, 33.*

Graves, L.M., & Powell, G.N. (1988). An investigation of sex discrimination in recruiters' evaluations of actual applicants. *Journal of Applied Psychology, 73,* 20-29.

Greenberg, J. (1986a). Determinants of perceived fairness of performance evaluations. *Journal of Applied Psychology,*

71, 340-342.

Greenberg, J. (1986b). Organizational performance appraisal procedures: What makes them fair? In R.J. Lewicki, B.H. Sheppard & M. Bazerman (Eds.), *Research on negotiation in organizations* (vol.1, pp.25-41). Greenwich, CT: JAI Press.

Greenberg, J. (1987a). A taxonomy of organizational justice theories. *Academy of Management Review*, 12, 9-22.

Greenberg, J. (1987b). Reactions to procedural injustice in payment distributions": Do the ends justify the means. *Journal of Applied Psychology*, 72, 340-342.

Greenberg, J. (1987c). Using diaries to promote procedural justice in performance appraisals. Social Justice Research, 1, 219-234.

Greenberg, J. (1989). Cognitive reevaluation of outcomes in response to underpayment inequity. *Academy of Management Journal*, 32, 174-184.

Greenberg, J. (1990a). Organizational justice: Yesterday, today and tomorrow. *Journal of Management*, 16, 399-432.

Greenberg, J. (1990b). Employee theft as a reaction to underpayment inequity: Hidden cost of pay cuts. *Journal of Applied Psychology*, 75, 561-568.

Greenberg, J., & Folger, R. (1983). Procedural justice, participation and the fair process effect in groups and organizations. In P.B. Paulus (Ed.), *Basic group process* (pp.235-256). New York: Springer-Verlag.

Griffeth, R.W., Vecchio, R.P., & Logan J.W. Jr. (1989). Equity theory and interpersonal attraction. *Journal of Applied Psychology*, 74, 394-410.

Griggs v. Duke Power Co. (1971). *Fair employment practices*, 175.

Groarke, L. (1990). Affirmative action as a form of restitution. *Journal of Business Ethics*, 9, 207-213.

Guion, R. (1987). Changing views for personnel selection research. *Personnel Psychology*, 40, 199-213.

Guion, R.M., & Gibson, W.M. (1988). Personnel selection and placement. *Annual Review of Psychology*, 39, 349-374.

Gurr, T.R. (1970). *Why men rebel. Princeton*, N.J.: Princeton University Press.

Haefner, J.E. (1977). Race, age, sex and competence as factors in employer selection of the disadvantaged. *Journal of Applied Psychology*, 62, 199-202.

Harris, M.M., & Fink, L.S. (1987). A fiels study of applicant reactions to employment opportunities: Does the recruiter make a difference? *Personnel Psychology*, 40, 765-784.

Hartigan, J.A., & Wigdor, A.K. (Eds.) (1989). *Fairness in*

employment testing. *Washington*, DC: National Academic Press.

Heilman, M.E. (1980).   The impact of situational factors on personnel decisions concerning women: Varying the sex composition of the applicant pool. *Organizational Behavior and Human Performance, 26,* 386-396.

Heilman, M.E., & Herlihy, J.M. (1984).   Affirmative action, negative reaction? Some moderating conditions. *Organisational Behaviour and Human Performance, 33,* 204-213.

Heilman, M.E., Lucas, J., & Kaplow, S. (1990).   Self-derogating consequences of sex-based preferential selection: The moderating role of initial self-confidence. *Organizational Behavior and Human Decision Processes, 46,* 202-216.

Heilman, M.E., & Martell, R. F. (1986). Exposure to successful women: Antidote to sex discrimination in applicant screening decisions. *Organizational Behavior and Human Decision Processes, 37,* 376-390.

Heilman, M.E., Rivero, J.C., & Brett, J.F. (1991).   Skirting the competence issue: Effects of sex-based preferential selection on task choices of women and men. *Journal of Applied Psychology, 76,* 99-105.

Heilman, M.E., Simon, M.C., & Repper, D.P. (1987).   Intentionally favored, unintentionally harmed?   Impact of sex-based preferential selection on self-perceptions and self-evaluations. *Journal of Applied Psychology, 72,* 62-68.

Herriot, P. (1989). Selection as a social process. In M. Smith & I.T. Robertson (Eds.), *Advances in selection and assessment.* (pp. 171-188). Chichester, England: Wiley.

Hitt, M.A., & Barr, S.H. (1989).   Managerial selection decision models: Examination of configural cue processing. *Journal of Applied Psychology, 74,* 53-61.

Hopper, R. (1977). Language attitudes in the employment interview. *Communication Monographs, 44,* 346-357.

Hopper, R., & Williams, F. (1973).   Speech characteristics and employability. *Speech Monographs, 4,* 296-302.

Hough, L.M. (1988). Development of personality measures to supplement selection decisions. Paper presented at the 24th Annual Confoerence of International Congress of Psychology, Sydney, Australia.

Howard, A. (1986). College experiences and managerial performance. *Journal of Applied Psychology, 71,* 530-552.

Hoyt, K.B. (1989). The career status of women and minority persons: A 20-year retrospective. *Career Development Quarterly, 37,*

202-212.

Hunter, J.E. (1980). *Test validation for 12000 jobs: An application of synthetic validity and validity generalization to the General Aptitude Test Battery (GATB).* Washington, DC: USEmployment Service, US Department of Labor.

Hunter, J.E. (1981). *Fairness of the GATB: Ability differences and their impact on minority hiring rates.* Washington, DC: US Employment Services, USDepartment of Labor.

Hunter, J.E. (1986). Cognitive ability cognitive aptitudes, job knowledge and job performance. *Journal of Vocational Behavior,* 29, 340-362.

Hunter, J.E., & Hunter, R. (1984). Validity and utility of alternative predictors. *Psychological Bulletin,* 96, 72-98.

Hunter, J.E., & Schmidt, F.L. (1976). Critical analysis of the statistical and ethical implications of various definitions of test bias. *Psychological Bulletin,* 83, 1053-1071.

Hunter, J.E., Schmidt, F.L., & Hunter, R. (1979). Differential validity of employment tests by race: A comprehensive review and analysis. *Psychological Bulletin,* 86, 721-735.

Hunter, J.E., Schmidt, F.L., & Raushenberger, J.M. (1977). Fairness of psychological tests: Implications of four definitions for selection utility and minority hiring. *Journal of Applied Psychology,* 62, 245-260.

Jackson, L.A. (1989). Relative deprivation and the gender wage gap. *Journal of Social Issues,* 45, 117-133.

Jacobson, M.B., & Koch, W. (1977). Women as leaders: Performance evaluation as a function of method of leader selection. *Organisational Behaviour and Human Performance,* 20, 149-157.

Janz, J.T. (1982). Initial comparisons of patterned behavior description interviews versus unstructured interviews. *Journal of Applied Psychology,* 67, 577-580.

Janz, J.T. (1987). The selection interview: The received wisdom versus recent research. In S. Dolan & R. Schuler (Eds.), *Canadian readings in personnel and human resource management.* St. Paul, MN: West.

Janz, J.T. (1988). Comparing the use and validity of opinions versus behavior descriptions in the employment interview. Unpublished manuscripts.

Janz, J.T. (1989). The patterned behavior description interview: The best prophet of the future is the past. In R.W. Eder & G.R. Ferris (Eds.), *The employment interview: Theory, research and practice.* London, Sage.

104

Janz, J.T., Hellervik, L., & Gilmore, D.C. (1986). *Behavior description interviewing: New accurate, cost effective.* Newton, MA: Allyn & Bacon.

Jenson, A.R. (1981). *Straight talk about mental tests.* New York: Free Press.

Jenson, A.R. (1985). The nature of the black-white difference on various psychometric tests: Spearman's hypothesis. *Behavioral and Brain Sciences, 8,* 193-219.

Jenson, A.R. (1986). G:Artifact or reality? *Journal of Vocational Behavior, 29,* 301-331.

Jones, E.E., & Nisbett, R.E. (1972). The actor and the observer: Divergent perceptions of the causes of behavior. in E.E. Jones & E.E. Kanouse, H.H. Kelley, R.E. Nisbett, S. Valins & B. Weiner (Eds.), *Attibution: Perceiving the causes of behavior.* Mrrristown, N.J. : General Learning Press.

Juster, F.T., & Courant, P.N. (1986). Integrating stocks and flows in quality of life research. In Andews, F.M. (Ed.), *Research on the quality of life.* Institute for Social Research, Ann Arbor, MI.

Kacmar, K.M., Ratcliff, S.L., & Ferris, G.R. (1989). Employment interview research: Internal and external validity. In R.W. Eder & G.R. Ferris (Eds.), *The employment interview.* London: Sage.

Kalin, R., & Rayko, D.S. (1978). Discrimination in evaluative judgments against foreign-accented job candidates. *Psychological Reports, 43,* 1203-1209.

Kanfer, R., Sawyer, J., Earley, P.C., & Lind, E.A. (1987). Participation in task evaluation procedures: The effect of influential opinion expression and knowledge of evaluative criteria on attitudes and performance. *Social Justice Research, 1,* 235-249.

Karambayya, R., & Brett, J.M. (1989). Managers handling disputes: Third party roles and perceptions of fairness. *Academy of Management Journal, 32,* 687-704.

Katzell, R.A., & Dyer, F.J. (1977). Differential validity revived. *Journal of Applied Psychology, 62,* 137-145.

Keenan, A. (1982). Candidate personality and performance in selection interviews. *Personnel Review, 11,* 20-22.

Key Business Directory of Australia (1990). Vol 1, Melbourne: Dun & Bradstreet International.

Kinder, D.R., & Sanders, L.M (1990). Mimicking political debate with survey questions: The case of white opinion on affirmative action for blacks. *Social Cognition, 8,* 73-103.

105

Kinicki, A.J., & Lockwood, C.A. (1985). The interview process: An examination of factors recuriters use in evaluating job applicants. *Journal kof Vocational Behavior, 26,* 117-125.

Kirkpatrick, J.J., Ewen, R.B., Barrett, R.S., & Katzell, R.A. (1968). *Testing and fair employment : Fairness and validity of personnel tests for different ethnic groups.* New York: New York University Press.

Kirnan, J.P., Farley, J.A., & Geisinger, K.F. (1989). The relationship between recuriting source, applicant quality and hire performance: An analysis by sex, ethnicity and age. *Personnel Psychology, 42,* 293-308.

Klaas, B.S. (1989). Determinants of grievance activity and the grievance system's impact on employee behavior: An integrative perspective. *Academy of Management Review, 32,* 705-717.

Kluegel, J.R., & Smith, E.R. (1983). Affirmative action attitudes: Effects of self-interest, racial affect and stratification beliefs on whites' views. *Spocial Forces, 61,* 797-824.

Koper, G., & Vermunt, R. (1988). The effects of procedural aspects and outcome salience on procedural fairness judgements. *Social Justice Research, 2,* 289-301.

Konovsky, M.A., & Cropanzano, R. (1991). Perceived fairness of employee drug testing as a predictor of employee attitudes and job performance. *Journal of Applied Psychology, 76,* 698-707.

Konovsky, M.A., & Folger, R. (1991). The effects of procedures, social accounts and benefits level on victim's layoff reactions. *Journal of Applied Social Psychology, 21,* 630-650.

Landy, F.J., Barnes, J.L., & Murphy, K.R. (1978). Correlates of perceived fairness and accuracy of performance evaluation. *Journal of Applied Psychology, 63,* 751-754.

Landy, F.J., Barnes-Farrell, J., & Cleveland, J.N. (1980). Perceived fairness and accuracy of performance evaluation: A follow-up. *Journal of Applied Psychology, 65,* 355-356.

Lane, R.E. (1988a). Book review of Lind and Tyler, The social psychology of procedural justice, *Social Justice Research, 2,* 309-317.

Lane, R.E. (1988b). Procedural goods in a democracy: How one is treated vs. what one gets. *Social Justice Research, 2,* 177-192.

Lansberg, I. (1989). Social categorization, entitlement and justice in organizations: Contextual determinants and cognitive underpinnings. *Human Relations, 41,* 871-899.

Latham, G.P., & Saari, L.M. (1984). Do people do what they say?

Further studies on the situational interview. *Journal of Applied Psychology, 69,* 569-573.

Latham, G.P., Saari, L.M., Pursell, E.D.,& Campion, M.A. (1980). The situational interview.*Journal of Applied Psychology, 65,* 442-431.

LaTour, S. (1978). Determinants of participant and observer satisfaction with adversary and inquisitorial modes of adjudication. *Journal of Personality and Social Psychology, 36,* 1531-1545.

Leonard, J.S. (1989). The changing face of employees and employment regulation. *California Management Review, 31,* 29-38.

Lerner, B. (1977). Washington v. Davis: Quantity, quality and equality in employment testing. In P. Kurland (Ed.), *The 1976 Supreme Court Review.* Chicago: University of Chicago Press.

Lerner, B. (1979). Employment discrimination: Adverse impact, validity and equality. In P. Kurland & G. Casper (Eds.), *The 1979 Supreme Court Review.* Chicago: University of Chicago Press.

Lerner, M.J. (1977). The justice motive: Some hypotheses as to its origins and forms. *Journal of Personality, 45,* 1-52.

Lerner, M.J. (1981). *The belief in a just world: A fundamental delusion.* New York: Plenum Press.

Lerner, M.J. (1982). The justice motive in human relations and the economic model of man: A radical analysis of facts and fictions. In V. Derlega & J. Grezlak (Eds.), *Cooperation and helping behavior: Theory and Research* (pp. 121-145).New York :Academic Press.

Leventhal, G.S. (1976). The distribution of rewards and resources in groups and organizations. In L.Berkowitz & E. Walster (Eds.),*Advances in experimental social psychology* (vol.9, pp.91-131) New York: Academic Press.

Leventhal, G.S. (1980). What should be done with equity theory? In K.J. Gergen, M.S. Greenberg, &R.H. Willis (Eds.), *Social exchange: Advances in theory and research* (pp.27-55). New York: Plenum.

Leventhal, G.S., Karuza, J., & Fry, W.R. (1980). Beyond fairness: A theory of allocation preferences. In G. Mikula(Ed.), *Justice and social interaction* (pp.167-218). New York: Springer-Verlag.

Lind, E.A., & Kanfer, R., & Earley, P.C. (1990). Voice, control and procedural justice: Instrumental and non-instrumental concerns in fairness judgements. *Journal of Personality and Social Psychology, 59,* 952-959.

Lind, E.A., Kurtz, S., Musante, L., Walker, L., & Thibaut, J.W. (1980). Procedure and outcome effects on reactions to adjudicated resolution of conflicts of interest. *Journal of Personality and Social Psychology, 39,* 643-653.

Lind, E.A., Lissak, R.I., & Conlon, D.E. (1983). Decision control and process control effects on procedural fairness judgements. *Journal of Applied Social Psychology, 13, 338-350.*

Lind, E.A., & Tyler, T.R. (1988). *The social psychology of procedural justice.* New York: Plenum Press.

Linn, R.L. (1978). Single-group validity , differential validity and differential predictions. *Journal of Applied Psychology, 63,* 507-514.

Lipset, S.M., & Schneider, W. (1978). The Bakke case: How would it be decided at the bar of public opinion? *Public Opinion, 1,* 38-44.

Lissak, R.I., Mendes, H., & Lind, E.A. (1983). Orgnaizational and ono-organizational influences on attitudes towards work. Unpublished manuscript, University of Illinios, Campaign.

Locke, E.A. (1986). *Generalizing from the laboratory to field settings: Research findings from industrial-organizational psychology* (pp.13-42). Lexington, MA:Lexington Books.

Locke, E., & Henne, D. (1986). Work motivation theories. In C.L. Cooper & I. Robertson (Eds.), *International Review of Industrial and Organizational Psychology,* pp.1-35. New York: Wiley.

Lopez, F.M., Jr.(1966). *Evaluating executive decision making.* American Management Association, Research Study 75. New York.

Love, K.G., & O'Hara, K.(1987). Predicting job performance of youth trainees under a job training partnership act program (JTPA): Criterion validation on a behavior-based measure of work maturity. *Personnel Psychology, 40,* 323-340.

Martin, J. (1981). Relative deprivation: A theory of distributive justice for an era of shrinking resources. In L.L. Cummings & B.M. Staw (Eds.), *Research in organizational behavior* (Vol. 3), p. 53-107. Greenwich, CT: JAI Press.

Martin, J., Price, R., Bies, R., & Powers, M. (1979, September). "Relative deprivation among secretaries: The effects of the token female executive" Paper presented at American Psychological Association, New York.

Maurer, S.D., & Fay, C. (1988). Effect of situational interviews, conventional structured interviews, and training on interview rating agreement: An experimental analysis. *Personnel Psychology*, 41

Mayor, Bylsma, & Cozzarelli, (1989). Gender differences in distributive justice preferences: The impact of domain. *Sex Roles*, 21, 487-497.

McDonald, T., & Hakel, M.D. (1985). Effects of applicant race, sex, suitability and answers on interviewer's questioning strategy and ratings. *Personnel Psychology*, 38, 321-334.

McEnrue, M.P. (1989). The perceived fairness of managerial promotion practices. *Human Relations*, 42, 815-827.

McEvoy, G.M., & Cascio, W.F. (1985). Strategies for reducing employee turnover. *Journal of Applied Psychology*, 70, 342-353.

McKinney, W.R. (1987). Public personnel selection: Issues and choice points: Public *Personnel Management Journal*, 16, 243-257.

Meglino, B.M., & DeNisi, A.S. (1987). Realistic job previews: Some thoughts on their more effective use in managing the flow of human resources. *Human Resources Planning*, 10, 157-167.

Meindl, J.R. (1989). Managing to be fair: An exploration of values, motives and leadership. *Administrative Science Quarterly*, 34, 252-276.

Messe, L.A., Hymes, R.W., & MacCoun, R.J. (1984). Minimal group membership and reward distribution behavior. Paper presented at American Psychological Association meeting, Toronto.

Miceli, M.P. (1985). The effects of realistic job previews on newcomer behavior: A laboratory study. *Journal of Vocational Behavior*, 26, 277-289.

Miles, E.W., Hatfield, J.D., & Huseman, R.C. (1989). The equity sensitivity construct: Potential implications for worker performance. *Journal of Management*, 15, 581-588.

Minas, A.C. (1977). How reverse discrimination compensates women. *Ethics*, 88, 74-79.

Miner, M.G. (1976). *Selection procedures and personnel records*. Washington, DC: Bureau of National Affairs.

Moore, D. (1990). Discrimination and deprivation: The effects of social comparisons, *Social Justice Research*, 4, 49-64.

Morrow, P.C., Mullen E.J., & McElroy, J.C. (1990). Vocational behavior 1989: The year in review. *Journal of Vocational Behavior*, 37, 121-195.

Mowday, R.T. (1987). Equity theory predictions of behavior in organizations. In R.M. Steers & L.W. Porter (Eds.), *Motivation and work behavior* (4th ed.), pp.89-110. New York: McGraw-Hill.

Mullins, T.W. (1982). Interviewer decisions as a function of applicant race, applicant quality, and interviewer prejudice. *Personnel Psychology, 35,* 161-174.

Nacoste, R.W. (1987). But do they care about fairness? The dynamics of preferential treatment and minority interest. *Basic and Applied Social Psychology, 8,* 177-191.

Nacoste, R.W.(1989). Affirmative action and self-evaluation. In F.A. Blanchard & F.J. Crosby (Eds.), *Affirmative action in perspective* (pp.103-109). New York: Springer-Verlag.

Nacoste, R.W., & Lehman, D (1987). Procedural stigma. *Representative Research in Social Psychology, 17,* 25-38.

Newton, L.H. (1973). Reverse discrimination as unjustified. *Ethics,* 83, 308-312.

Noe, R.A., & Steffy, B.D. (1987). The influence of individual characteristics and asessment center evaluation on career exploration behavior and job involvement. *Journal of Vocational Behavior, 30,* 187-202.

Norvell, N., & Worchel, S. (1981). A re-examination of the relation between equal status contact and intergroup attraction. *Journal of Personality and Social Psychology, 41,* 902-908.

O'Connor, E.J., Wexley, K.N., & Alexander, R.A. (1975). Single group validity: Fact or fallacy? *Journal of Applied Psychology, 60,* 352-355.

Olian, J.D., Schwab, D.P., & Haberfeld, Y. (1988). The impact of applicant gender compared to qualifications on hiring recommendations: A meta-analysis of experimental studies. *Organizational Behavior and Human Decision Process, 41,* 180-195.

Optow, S. (1987). Modifying the scope of justice: An experimental examination. Paper presented at the American Psychological Association meeting, New York.

Optow, S. (1988). Outside the realm of fairness: Aspects of moral exclusion. Paper presented at American Psychological Association meeting, Atlanta.

Parsons, C.K., & Liden, R.C. (1984). Interviewer perceptions of applicant qualifications: A multivariate field study of demographic characteristics and nonverbal cues. *Journal of Applied Psychology, 69,* 557-568.

Paunonen, S.V., Jackson, D.N., & Aberman, S.M. (1987). Personnel selection decisions: Effects of applicant personality and the letter of reference. *Organisational Behavior and Human Decision Processes, 40,* 96-114.

Pearn, M.A. (1989). Fairness in employment selection:A comparison of UK and USA experience. In M. Smith & I.T. Robertson (Eds.), *Advances in selection and assessment, pp. 154-163.* New York: Wiley.

Peters, R.J. (1987). *Practical intelligence.* New York: Harper& Row.

Peterson, N.S., & Novick, M.R. (1976). An evaluation of some models for culture-fair selection. *Journal of Educational Measurement, 13,* 3-29.

Pettigrew, T. F. (1958). The measurement and correlates of category width as a cognitive variable. *Journal of Personality, 26,* 532-544.

Pettigrew, T. (1967). Social evaluation theory. In D. Levine (Ed.), *Nebraska symposium on motivation* (vol. 15). Lincoln:University of Nebraska Press.

Pettigrew, T. (1978). Three issues in ethnicity: Boundaries, deprivations, and perceptions. In J.M. Yinger & S.J. Cutler (Eds.), *Major social issues: A multidisciplinary view.* New York: Free Press.

Pettigrew, T., & Martin, J. (1987). Shaping the organizational context for black American inclusion. *JOurnal of Social Issues, 43,* 41-78.

Phillips, A.P., & Dipboye, R.L. (1989). Correlational tests of predictions from a process model of the interview. *Journal of Applied Psychology, 74,* 41-52.

Ponder, D.G. (1987). Testing the generalizability of bias in teacher selection ratings across different modes of screening. *Journal of Educational Equity and Leadership.7,* 49-59.

Powell, G.N. (1987). The effects of sex and gender on recruitment. *Academy of Management Review, 12,* 731-743.

Premack, S.J., & Wanous, J.P. (1985). A meta-analysis of realistic job preview experiments. *Journal of Applied Psychology, 70,* 706-719.

Pulakos, E.D., Borman, W.C., & Hough, L.M. (1988). Test validation for scientific understanding: Two demonstrations of an approach to studying predictor-criterion linkages. *Personnel Psychology, 41,* 703-716.

Pursell, E.D., Campion, M.A., & Gaylord, S.R. (1980). Structured interviewing: Avoiding selection problems. *Personnel Journal, 59,* 907-912.

Raju, N.S., & Burke, M.J. (1983). Two new procedures for studying validity generalization. *Journal of Applied Psychology, 68,* 382-395.

Rawls, J. (1971). *A theory of justice.* Cambridge, MA: Harvard University Press.

Reis, H.T. (1986). Levels of interest in the study of interpersonal justice. In H.W. Bierhoff, R.L. Cohen & J. Greenberg (Eds.), *Justice in social relations.* (pp.187-209). New York: Plenum.

Rhodebeck, L. (1981). Group deprivation: An alternative model for explaining collective political action. *Micropolitics, 1,* 239-267.

Robertson, I.T, & Smith, M. (1989). Personnel selection methods. In M.Smith & I.T. Robertson (Eds.), *Advances in selection and assessment.* (pp.89-112). Chichester, England: Wiley.

Rothstein, M., & Jackson, D.N. (1984). Implicit personality theory and the employment interview. In M. Cook (Ed.), *Issues in person perception.* London:Methuen.

Rousseau, D.M., & Anton, R.J. (1988). Fairness and implied contract obligations in termination: A policy capturing study. *Human Performance, 1,* 273-289.

Runciman, W.G. (1966). *Relative deprivation and social justice: A study of attitudes to social inequality in twentieth-century England.* Berkeley, CA: University of California Press.

Runciman, W.G. (1968). Problems of research on relative deprivation. In H.H. Hyman & E. Singer (Eds.), *Readings in reference group theory and research.* New York: Free Press.

Schmidt, F.L. (1988). The problem of group differences in ability test scores in employment selection. *Journal of Vocation Behavior, 33,* 272-293.

Schmidt, F.L., Berner, J.G., & Hunter, J.E. (1973). Racial differences in validity of employment tests: Reality or illusion? *Journal of Applied Psychology, 53,* 5-9.

Schmidt, F.L., & Hunter, J.E. (1974). Racial and ethnic bias in psychological tests. *American Psychologist, 29,* 1-9.

Schmidt, F.L., & Hunter, J.E. (1983). Individual differences in productivity: An empirical test of estimates derived from studies of selection procedure utility. *Journal of Applied Psychology, 68,* 407-414.

Schmidt, F.L., Hunter, J.E., McKenzie, R.C., & Muldrow, T.W. (1979). Impact of valid selection procedures on work-force productivity. *Journal of Applied Psychology, 64,* 609-626.

Schmidt, F.L., Hunter, J.E., & Pearlman, K. (1981). Task differences and validity of aptitude tests in selection: A red herring. *Journal of Applied Psychology, 66,* 166-185.

Schmidt, F.L., Hunter, J.E., Pearlman, K., & Hirsh, H.R. (1985). Forty questions about validity generalization and meta-analysis. *Personnel Psychology, 38,* 697-798.

Schmidt, F.L., Mack, M.J., & Hunter, J.E. (1984). Selection utility in the occupation of US Park Ranger for three modes of test use. *Journal of Applied Psychology, 69,* 490-497.

Schmidt, F.L., Ones, D.S., & Hunter, J.E. (1992). Personnel selection. *Annual Review of Psychology, 43,* 627-670.

Schmidt, F.L., Pearlman, K., & Hunter, J.E. (1980). The validity and fairness of employment and educational tests for Hispanic Americans: A review and analysis. *Personnel Psychology, 33,* 705-724.

Schmitt, N. (1989). Fairness in employment selection. In M. Smith & Robertson, I. (Eds.), *Advances in personnel selection and assessment,* p.133-152. Chichester: Wiley.

Schmitt, N., & Noe, R.A. (1986). Personnel selection and equal employment opportunity. In C.L. Cooper, & I.T. Robertson (Eds.), *International review of industrial and organizational psychology.* New York: Wiley.

Schmitt, N., & Robertson, I. (1990). Personnel selection. *Annual Review of Psychology, 41,* 289-319.

Sears, D., & McConahay, J. (1970). Racial socialization, comparison levels and the Watts Riot. *Journal of Social Issues, 26,* 121-140.

Senchak, M., & Reis, H.T. (1988). The fair process effect and procedural criteria in the resolution of inputs between intimate same-sex friends. *Social Justice Research, 2,* 263-287.

Sharf, J.C. (1988).Litigating personnel measurement policy. In L.S. Gottfredson & J.C. Sharf (Eds.), Fairness in employment testing. *Journal of Vocational Behavior, 33,* 235-271.

Shaw, B. (1988). Affirmative action: An ethical evaluation. Journal of Business Ethics, 7, 763-770.

Sheppard, B.H. (1984). Third party conflict intervention: A procedural framework. In B.M. Staw & L.L. Cummings (Eds.), *Research in organizational behavior* (Vol. 6, pp.141-190). Greenwich, CT: JAI Press.

Sheppard, B.H., & Lewick, R.J. (1987). Toward general principles of managerial fairness. *Social Justice Research, 1,* 161-176.

Sher, G. (1975). Justifying reverse discrimination in employment. *Philosophy and Public Affairs, 4,* 159-170.

Singer, M.S. (1988). The effect of applicant ethnicity on selection decisions: Are results generalizable from resume to interview research? *Australian Journal of Psychology*, 40, 423-431.

Singer, M.S. (1990a). Determinants of perceived fairness in selection practices: An organizational justice perspective. *Genetic, General and Social Psychology Monographs*, 116, 475-494.

Singer, M.S. (1990b). Preferential selection and outcome justice: Effects of justification and merit discrepancy. *Social Justice Research*, 4, 285-305.

Singer, M.S. (1990c). Individual differences in category width and fairness perception of selection decisions. *Social Behavior and Personality: An International Journal.* 18, 87-94.

Singer, M.S. (1992a). Procedural justice in managerial selection: Identification of fairness determinants and consequences of fairness perceptions. *Social Justice Research*, 5, 49-70.

Singer, M.S. (1992b). The application of relative deprivation theory to justice perception of preferential selection. *Current Psychology: Research and Reviews*, 11, 128-144.

Singer, M.S. (1992c). Gender-based preferential selection: Perceptions of injustice and empathy of deprivation. *Applied Psychology: An International Review*, (under revision)

Singer, M.S., & Bruhns, C. (1991). Relative effect of applicant work experience and academic qualification on selection interview decisions: A study of between-sample generalizability. *Journal of Applied Psychology*, 76, 550-559..

Singer, M.S., & Sowell, C. (1989). Applicant age and selection interview decisions: Effects of information exposure on age discrimination in personnel selection. *Personnel Psychology*, 42, 135-154.

Smith, M. (1989). Some British data concerning the standard deviation of performance. *Journal of Occupational Psychology*, 62, 189-190.

Soltan, K. E. (1987). *The causal theory of justice.* Berkeley, CA: University of California Press.

Snyderman, M., & Rothman, S. (1986). Science, politics and the IQ controversy. *The Public Interest*, 83, 79-98.

Steffy, B.D., & Ledvinka, J. (1989). The long-range impact of five definitions of "fair" employee selection on black employment and employee productivity. *Organizational Behavior and Human Decision Processes*, 44, 297-324.

Stephan, W.G. (1985). Intergroup relations. In G. Lindzey, & E. Aronson (Eds.), *The Handbook of social psychology* (Vol.2, 3rd ed.) p.599-658. New York: Random House.

114

Sullivan, T. A. (1989). Women and minority workers in the new economy: optimistic, pessimistic and mixed scenarios. *Work and Occupations*, 16, 393-415.

Sweeney, P.D., McFarlin, D.B., & Cotton, L (1991). Locus of control as a moderator of the relationship between perceived influence and procedural justice. *Human Relations*, 44, 333-342.

Sweeney, P. D., McFarlin, D.B., & Inderrieden, E.J. (1990). Using relative deprivation theory to explain satisfaction with income and pay level: A multistudy examination. *Academy of Management Journal*, 33, 423-436.

Tajfel, H. (1982). *Social identity and intergroup relations.* Cambridge: Cambridge University Press.

Tajfel, H., & Turner, J. (1979). An integrative theory of intergroup conflict. In W.G. Austin & S. Worchel (Eds.), *The social psychology of intergroup relations* . Monterey, CA: Brooks/Cole.

Taylor, M.S., & Bergmann, T.J. (1987). Organizational recruitment activities and applicants' reactions at different stages of the recruitment process. *Personnel Psychology*, 40, 261-286.

Taylor, P.W. (1973). Reverse discrimination and compensatory justice. *Analysis*, 33, 177-182.

Thibaut, J. & Walker, L. (1975). *Procedural justice: A psychological analysis.* Hillsdale, NJ: Erlbaum.

Thibaut, J., & Walker, L. (1978). *A theory of procedure.* California Law Review, 66, 541-566.

Thorndike, R.L. (1971). Concepts of culture fairness, *Journal of Educational Measurement*, 8, 63-70.

Thorndike, R.L. (1986). The role of general ability in prediction. *Journal of Vocational Behavior*, 29, 332-339.

Title VII of the Civil Rights Act of 1964, pp. 703(a), 42 U.S.C. 2000e.

Tosi, H.L., & Einbender, S.W. (1985). The effects of the type and amount of information in sex discrimination research: A meta-analysis. *Academy of Management Review*, 28, 712-723.

Tougas, F., Beaton, A.M., & Veilleux, F. (1991). Why women approve of affirmative action: The study of a predictive model. *International Journal of Psychology*, 26, 761-776.

Tougas, F.L., Dube, L., & Veilleux, F. (1987). Privation relative et programmes d'action positive. *Revue Canadienne des Sciences du Comportement*, 19, 167-176.

Tougas, F.L., & Veilleux, F. (1988). The influence of identification, collective relative deprivation and procedure of implementation on women's responses to affirmative action: A causal modeling approach. *Canadian Journal of Behavioral Sciences, 20,* 16-29.

Tougas, F.L., & Veilleux, F. (1989). Who likes affirmative action: Attitudinal processes among men and women. In F.A. Blanchard & F.C. Crosby (Eds), *Affirmative action in perspective.* (pp. 111-124). New York: Springer-Verlag.

Tougas, F.L., Veilleux, F., Cere, M., & Boudreault, L. (1989). L'effet de I'information sur la privation relative collective dans une situation d'evaluation de candidates, *Revue Quebecoise de Psychologie, 10,* 1-12.

Tsalikis, J., & Ortiz-Buonafina, M. (1990). Ethical beliefs' differences of males and females. *Journal of Business Ethics, 9,* 509-517.

Tversky, A., & Kahneman, D. (1981). The framing of decisions and the psychology of choice. *Science, 211,* 453-458.

Tyler, T.R. (1987). Conditions leading to value expressive effects in judgements of procedural justice: A test of four models. *Journal of Personality and Social Psychology, 52,* 333-344.

Tyler, T.R., & Bies, R.J. (1990). Beyond formal procedures: The interpersonal context of procedural justice. In J. Carroll (Ed.), *Applied social psychology and organizational settings* (pp. 77-98), Hillsdale, NJ: Erlbaum.

Tyler, T.R., & Lind, E.A. (1990). Intrinsic versus community-based justice models: When does group membership matter. *Journal of Social Issues, 46,* 83-94.

Tyler, T.R., Rasinski, K., & Spodick, N. (1985). The influence of voice on satisfaction with leaders: Exploring the meaning of process control. *Journal of Personality and Social Psychology, 48,* 72-81.

Uniform Guidelines on Employee Selection Procedures (1978). *Federal Register, 43,* 38290-38315.

Vanneman, R., & Pettigrew, T. (1972). Race and relative deprivation in the United States. *Race, 13,* 461-486.

Vaughan, G.M., & Corballis, M.C. (1969). Beyond tests of significance: Estimating strength of effects in selected ANOVA designs. *Psychological Bulletin, 72,* 204-213.

Veilleux, F., & Tougas, F. (1989). Male acceptance of affirmative action programs for women: The results of altruistic or egoistical motives. *International Journal of Psychology, 24,* 485-496.

Venneman, R., & Pettigrew, T. (1972). Race and relative deprivation in the urban United States. *Race, 13,* 461-486.

Walster, E., Berscheid, E., & Walster, G.W. (1973). New directions in equity research. *Journal of Personality and Social Psychology, 25,* 151-176.

Walster, W., & Walster, E.H. (1975). Equity and social justice. *Journal of Social Issues, 31,* 21-44.

Wanous, J.P. (1980). *Organizational entry: Recruitment, selection and socialization of newcomers.* Reading, MA: Addison-Wesley.

Wanous, J.P. (1989). Installing a realistic job preview: Ten tough choices. *Personnel Psychology, 42,* 117-134.

Weekley, J.A., & Gier, J.A. (1987). Reliability and validity of the situational interview for a sales position. *Journal of Applied Psychology, 72,* 484-487.

Wegener, B. (1990). Equity, relative deprivation and the value consensus paradox. Social Justice Research, 4 , 65-86.

Weick, K.E. (1966). The concept of equity in the perception of pay. *Administrative Science Quarterly, 11,* 414-439.

Whiddon, B., & Martin, P.Y. (1989). Organizational democracy and work quality in a state welfare agency. *Social Science Quarterly, 70,* 667-686.

White, S.W. (1988). Opportunity and intelligence. *The Phi Kappa Phi Journal, 68,* 2-3.

Wiesner, W.H., & Cronshaw, S.F. (1988). A meta-analytic investigation of the impact of interview format and degree of structure on the validity of the employment interview. *Journal of Occupational Psychology, 61,* 275-290.

Wigdor, A.K., & Garner, W.R. (1982). *Ability testing: Uses consequences and controversies.* Washington DC: Academy Press.

Wigdor, A.K., & Hartigan, J.A. (1988). *Interim report: Within-group scoring of the General Aptitude Test Battery,* Washington DC: Academy Press.

Young, I. P. & Allison, B. (1982). Effects of candidate age and teaching experience on school superintendents and principals in in selection teachers. *Planning and Changing, 13,* 245-256.

Young, I.P., & Ponder, D.G. (1985). Salient factors affecting decision making in simulated teacher selection interviews. *Journal of Educational Equity and Leadership, 5,* 216-233.

Young, I.P., & Voss, G. (1986). Effects of chronological age, amount of information and type of teaching position on administrators' perceptions of teacher candidates, *Journal of Educational Equity and Leadership, 6,* 27-44.

Index